I0814713

HOW A DIVINE MIND WORKS

HOW A DIVINE MIND WORKS

RELEASING THE POWER FOR UNCOMMON SUCCESS & SPIRITUAL GROWTH

Thomas Lacy

Carpenter's Son Publishing

Published by Carpenter's Son Publishing
Carpentersonpublishing.com

Cover Design by Clementine Bowers

Interior Design by Suzanne Lawing

Printed in the United States of America

ISBN: 978-1-956370-47-8 (print)

Dedication

This book is dedicated to my late brother, James A. Lacy. We had several conversations about various content in this book. He had a master's degree in psychology, and he looked forward to the completion of this literary work with great anticipation. Unfortunately, he passed away and went home to heaven before this publishing. With love, respect, and admiration, I dedicate this book to his memory.

I also dedicate this book to my late parents, Rev. Dr. Thomas A. Lacy Sr. and Mrs. Louise Lacy. I am grateful for what they imparted into my life that has contributed to my early spiritual development, growth, and success in life. I thank God for my parents, who trained me as a child in the way I should go, and as I grew older, I did not depart from that parental training and godly rearing.

Acknowledgments

First and foremost, I give glory and honor to God. Thank You, Jesus, for the Holy Spirit who has inspired me to write this book and has gifted, instructed, directed, and guided me along the way on the long journey to the completion of the same.

I also want to thank my wife, Dr. Constance Lacy (PhD, LCSW, HS–BCP), licensed clinical therapist, for her love, support, and endurance through eight years of the writing and publishing process that involved multiple short-term sabbaticals.

I want to recognize and thank my senior pastor Michael Hankins, who passed away in 2021, for being a sounding board and an encouraging source of support.

And last but not least, I want to acknowledge all of my friends, classmates, coworkers, and various professional associates with whom I have had discussions regarding some of the content in this book. Their receptivity and encouragement has meant a lot to me, and I am eternally grateful.

Contents

Author's Initial Testimony—1984

The book entitled *How a Divine Mind Works* has been written as a result of my experience and many testimonies, which were documented in a journal for over thirty years.

My exposure to—and application of—the power of the mind, especially the subconscious mind, has resulted in higher levels of success in multiple careers and business ventures.

This journey began in 1980 as I read and studied books such as *The Magic of Thinking Big, Think and Grow Rich, The Power of Your Subconscious Mind, The Magic of Believing,* and my Bible for God's promises, of course.

Testimony

While employed as an engineer for a Fortune 100 technology company, I observed that this mammoth household-name company did not have a quality manual for their Power Systems Division. I was a senior quality engineer with about ten years of experience in this specialized discipline. I was accustomed to working on government contracts and aerospace projects with other Fortune 100 technology companies in their quality departments that already had quality manuals and quality procedures documented.

When I realized that the current company that I was working for did not have a quality manual documented and issued, I saw and seized the opportunity to practice some of what I had been reading and studying about.

So I decided to write a letter to the director of engineering to address my observation and concerns. I built a case and presented a needs analysis. Along with the letter, I attached a copy of my personal resume. In that letter, I suggested that I was the most qualified person to manage the project to design, develop, and document the Power Systems Division quality manual. In the process, I basically created a new position and title for myself, as my proposal was accepted and approved.

Because of the work I did in that newly created position, I was nominated by the company division Engineering Universe at Large and was recognized as the Engineer of the Year for Professional Contribution. That award came with a couple of really nice gifts, of which one was monetary.

Now I do not share this testimony to impress you but rather to impress upon you that the information in this book has the potential to produce a thousand times the results I experienced back in 1984. My hope is that this book will transform the lives of everyone who reads it and bring them into a clearer understanding of God's supreme purpose for their Divine Mind. May the quality of your life be enhanced exponentially by the content of this book, and may blessings abound to you.

Introduction

For more than three decades, I have read, studied, and practiced various aspects of success principles including self-improvement, self-motivation, self-help, the subconscious mind, and the power of believing. For eight years, I have explored, researched, studied, and documented the significance of understanding the mind and how it works. But more significantly, a *Divine Mind.* Understanding what it is and how it works is of paramount importance to Christians. Because without that knowledge and understanding, one will be confused by the immensely complex, complicated, and divinely integrated system that God designed and created. This book is an attempt to uncomplicate things and empower you to be who God wants you to be. It will help you to "think right for your life type."

Most of the human confusion and scriptural misunderstanding comes from the use of the words "mind," "heart," "soul," and "spirit." These words are often used in scripture on an interchangeable basis, thus creating deeper confusion. This confusion is compounded by the complexity of the English language with its multiple spellings for the same sounding words with different meanings. It has also resulted in far too much fuzzy thinking regarding our spiritual expectations.

First Corinthians 14:33 (NKJV) tells us that God is not the author of confusion, so, by default, that leaves Satan, who is the father of lies and author of confusion. In the area of the mind, Satan thrives on lies and confusion, and craftily uses them to his advantage. That's because Satan knows and understands what a lot of Christians don't know and understand. He knows that our mind is the key to how we live and move and have our being. Satan knows that if he can just keep Christians confused and lacking knowledge and understanding about their own mind, such as what it is, where it is, how it works, and God's purpose for it, then they will continue to operate in their own human mind rather than the mind of Christ. Hence, they will remain conformed to this world and not transformed from it.

Man is comprised of spirit, soul, and body (see 1 Thessalonians 5:23). Spirit is not who you are. spirit is *what* you are. The same spirit that is in Christ Jesus is in you and me. We are one spirit with Christ.

Soul is *who* you are! Most Christians have heard that your soul consists of your mind, your will, and your emotions.

Nothing identifies you more than your soul. Your soul houses or is resident to your character, your integrity, and your intentions as well as your thoughts, opinions, and beliefs. The heart also comes into play here with a relationship to the mind.

The only part of your being that is physical is your body. Your body is a molecular structure that vibrates at a very high frequency. Your spirit—or you as a spirit—is not physical.

Your soul is not physical either. You cannot handle it, pick it up and move it around, or even see it with the natural physical eye. Your will is not physical, and your emotions are not physical. Nor is your mind physical. These nonphysical aspects of your being are not tangible. They are intangible!

Everything that is a part of your human body is physical. Surgeons can cut someone open, and everything inside of their body is physical. It can be moved and removed. Surgeons can touch it and handle it. In addition, you have absolutely no manual control over the biological functions that take place in your physical body. Your brain controls certain functions that operate in the body. It is the operating system, like that of a computer (or more like a control panel). Your mind is the software. A computer without software is useless. The brain and mind work together. The mind controls the brain and the brain controls the body. The mind manifests healing. It created your body. The mind also maintains, repairs, changes, and renews your body.

Your brain is physical. Your mind is not. Your mind is mental, thus intangible. So everything about you that is physical and nonphysical is controlled or influenced by your mind. Your mind is the most powerful aspect of you. We will look into scriptures that validate much that has been overlooked and not addressed or not taught in the Christian sector, the church, and the faith-based communities at large (in my humble opinion). So get ready to tighten up your seat belt and put on your oxygen mask, because we are getting ready to dive deeper and fly higher than ever before through the integration/acquisition of knowledge and understanding, and there will be revelation that comes forth. Wisdom is the principal thing. Therefore, get wisdom; and in all your getting, get understanding. Because without understanding, there is no revelation (see Proverbs 4:7).

By the way, where does wisdom reside? God said if we ask for wisdom, He will give it to us. But how do we receive it, and where does it go or where does God put it when He gives wisdom to us? You see, wisdom is another one of those nonphysical, intangible, mentally related intellectual aspects of our being.

I submit to you that any nonphysical aspect of our lives is channeled through or resides in the mind. And not only that, but even the physical things in your life, outside of your body, are also influenced by your mind. As you will see, scriptures validate and prove it to be so.

The body is the entire biological or physical part of a person. In the first chapter of Genesis, God said, "Let Us make man in Our image, according to Our likeness; and let them rule over the fish of the sea and over the birds of the sky and over the cattle and over all the earth, and over every creeping thing that creeps on the earth" (see Genesis 1:26–28 NASB 1995). God created man in His own image. In the image of God, He created them: male and female.

According to the Bible, mankind is distinct from all the rest of creation, including the animals, in that man is made in the image of God. As God is a tripartite—Father, Son, and Holy Spirit—man is also three parts: spirit, soul, and body. Man is made up of physical matter: the body, which can be seen and touched. But man is also made up of nonmaterial aspects, which are intangible. These include the mind, spirit, and heart. These nonmaterial aspects exist beyond the physical realm and lifespan of the human body and are therefore eternal. These nonmaterial aspects—the spirit, soul, heart, conscious, mind, and emotions—make up the personality of man. The Bible makes it clear that the soul and spirit are the primary nonmaterial aspects of humanity, while the body is the physical container. As human beings, we live eternally as a spirit.

I want to encourage you to read and study this book as if your life depended on it, because it very well may. If it is not your life depending on it, then it could be your quality of life, for sure.

We only have one mind. It consists of three parts, each of which operates in a different way. The three parts are the conscious, the subconscious, and the unconscious.[1] God designed all three parts to work together completely for His purpose and His glory. We call it a Divine Mind. Understanding how it works is paramount. It is a fact that your thoughts, beliefs, words, and deeds are a critical part of what determines your wealth, health, happiness, and success in life.

God gave us our mind for His purpose! It is the most powerful aspect of our being, and it connects us to God and allows Him to communicate to us and with us at all times. Your Divine Mind keeps you in perpetual oneness with God. Understanding how your mind works, especially your Divine Mind, will absolutely empower you!

Be prepared to discover amazing biblical truths through scriptures (BCV—book, chapter, and verse[2]) that have not been taught widely enough. I believe that what you are about to learn will take your relationship with our Heavenly Father to an all-time highest level and will be most pleasing to Him.

I pray that this book will be a blessing to you and instrumental in helping you to renew your mind for the transforming of your life.

CHAPTER 1:

Mind Connection

Let's dive a little deeper into all of this. I am going to make a statement that we will later let the Word of God validate. Okay?

Your mind is the connector to the universe, God, and the Holy Spirit. Your mind is the link that connects you to the One Universal Mind . . . the *Master's* mind (not associated with or to be confused with any mastermind group that individuals may organize as a peer-to-peer mentoring group used to help members solve their problems with input and advice from other group members).

What you draw or attract into your life, and what you put out or send out into the universe, is streamed through your mind and your mouth. And remember that the three parts of your mind each have a separate function and operate differently. But they do work together, whether on purpose or by default. This is God's mind design, and this is how He made us. It is truly so awesome!

Have you ever said what was on your mind? Well, God did. In the book of Genesis, we see that "God said" something ten times, and we can also read where reference is made to "God said" in both the Old and New Testaments.[1] Actually, God said what was in His mind, not what was *on* His mind. He verbalized His thoughts. We are able to do the same thing because we are made in His likeness.

You are going to get to a level of understanding that will revolutionize your life and create a paradigm shift in your thinking. You will discover how much of your life has not been fulfilled due to a lack of knowledge. The Word of God says in Hosea 4:6 (KJV), "My people are destroyed for lack of knowledge." The good news is that we can reverse the destruction with the acquisition of knowledge.

Remember: you are a spirit, you have a soul, and you live in a body. In 1 Thessalonians 5:23 (ISV) we read, "May the God of peace Himself make you holy in every way. And may your whole being—spirit, soul, and body—remain blameless when our Lord Jesus, the Messiah, appears."

In order to operate successfully, each of these three parts must be fed properly. The soul feeds on intellectual food to produce intellectual strength. The body feeds on physical food to produce physical strength. The spirit—the heart or inner man—is the real you, the part that has been reborn in Christ Jesus. It must feed on spiritual food, God's Word, in order to produce and develop faith. God said He will put His laws in our hearts and minds. He very much wants us to understand His declaration that He put it in scripture three times and in two different ways:

> "This is the covenant I will make with the people of Israel after that time," declares the Lord. "I will put my law in their minds and write it on their hearts. I will be their God, and they will be my people."
> —Jeremiah 31:33 NIV

> "This is the covenant I will make with them after that time," says the Lord. "I will put my laws in their hearts, and I will write them on their minds."
> —Hebrews 10:16

> "This is the covenant I will establish with the people of Israel after that time," declares the Lord. "I will put my laws in their minds and write them on their hearts, I will be their God, and they will be my people."
> —Hebrews 8:10

As we feast upon God's Word, our minds become renewed, and we have a fresh mental perspective and spiritual attitude.

God's Word, this spiritual food, enters our mind, takes root in our hearts, is formed by our tongue, and spoken out of our mouths. This is a powerful creative process! The spoken word has power as we declare it and apply the action to it.

Prayer based upon the Word rises above the human senses, even the conscious mind. It contacts the Author of the Word (the Author and Finisher of our faith) and sets His spiritual laws into motion. It is not just saying a prayer that gets the results, but it is the power of believing that produces results.

> If you can believe, all things are possible to him who believes.
> —Mark 9:23 NKJV

> For with the heart one believes unto righteousness, and with the mouth confession is made unto salvation.
> —Romans 10:10

Be Renewed in the Spirit of Your Mind

Behind the behavior, actions, attitudes, emotions, and habits are ways of thinking that encourage and strengthen them. They are established by one's mindset. To bring about deep change, we must change the way we think: our perspective or the way we see and perceive things.

The heart is a kind of storage bin where ways of thinking develop based on what is kept and cultivated in it. Read below what Jesus had to say about the abundance of the heart:

> How can you, being evil, speak good things? For out of the abundance of the heart the mouth speaks. A good man out of the good treasure of his heart brings forth good things, and an evil man out of the evil treasure brings forth evil things. . . . For by your words you will be justified, and by your words you will be condemned.
> —Matthew 12:34b, 35, 37

Transformation of life is a matter of the heart and mind combined. To change behavior, attitudes and emotions, we must challenge perspectives and mindsets and start seeing things from a positive viewpoint.

One of the most positive things one can experience is peace of mind. True peace comes from God, because God is our peace, as the Hebrew phrase *Jehovah-Shalom* expresses "The-LORD-*Is*-Peace" in Judges 6:24. In the presence of God, change is available.

You will keep him in perfect peace, Whose mind is stayed on You, Because he trusts in You.
—Isaiah 26:3

God's Work of Transformation

Allow God to transform you by His Word and by changing the way you think. God works to transform us at the deepest level, and He has supplied the means within our mind.

The mind and the brain are not the same! Contrary to the popular belief of many, thinking does not take place in your brain. So let's talk about the functions of your brain.

CHAPTER 2:

Brain vs. Mind

What the Brain *Is*

The brain is an organ that serves as the center of the nervous system in all vertebrate and most invertebrate animals. The brain is located in the head. Physiologically, the function of the brain is to exert centralized control over the other organs of the body. The brain acts on the rest of the body by generating patterns of muscle activity and by driving the secretion of chemicals called hormones.

The brain is the organ that controls the functions of the body. It is sometimes referred to as a muscle of thinking as the brain actually tells your muscles what to do. The brain is the most important organ in the body because it controls all of the bodily functions as well as the other organs, including the complete nervous system and chemical balances within the body. In addition to being the most important organ in the body, it is also the most complex organ in the body. One might say that it is the head organ . . . pun intended, but not because it is located in the head.

The brain is made up of a complex network of possibly 100 *billion* neutrons, each of which connects to up to 10,000 (typically) other neutrons. By some estimates, there are over 100 *trillion* total connection points in the human brain. The typical brain weighs only three pounds, but it is the source of most qualities that make you who you are. Neurons in the brain and spinal cord are part of the nervous system and act as a body's "command central."

The brain is constantly active, even when we are asleep. As a matter of fact, asleep or awake, the brain requires 20 percent of the heart's output of fresh blood and 20 percent of the blood's oxygen and glucose to keep functioning properly. Glucose is a type of sugar that is our brain's primary fuel. The brain produces enough electrical energy to power a 40-watt light bulb for twenty-four hours. That is a lot of energy for a human organ that is a little bigger than a softball.[1] There is a mixed school of thought regarding some brain science facts and statistics, but they all make for interesting dialogue.

Only God could design such a magnificent, powerful, and awesome creation as the human brain.

Some Interesting Brain Facts

- Sixty percent of your brain is fat. Note: There was a jazz and rhythm and blues saxophonist who worked alongside Ray Charles, whose name was David *Fathead* Newman. That is a fact. So if someone ever calls you a "lardhead," don't get mad. They are just stating a fact (LOL).

- In 2015, the fourth most powerful supercomputer in the world took forty minutes to simulate just one second of human brain activity.
- Every time you recall a memory or have a new thought, you are creating a new connection in your brain (a.k.a. auto system updates).
- A piece of brain tissue the size of a grain of sand contains 100,000 neurons and 1 billion synapses, all communicating with each other.
- More than 100,000 chemical reactions take place in your brain every second.
- Your brain storage capacity is considered virtually unlimited. It does not get "used up" like random access memory (RAM) in your laptop computer.
- There are about four miles of blood vessels in the brain.
- Although pain is processed in your brain, your brain has no pain receptors and feels no pain. This explains how brain surgery can be performed while the patient is awake with no pain or discomfort.[2]

What the Brain Is *Not*

The brain is *not* the mind. The brain is tangible, and the mind is intangible. The brain is physical in nature, and the mind is mental/intellect. The brain and the mind are not the same! Each has its own purpose and function. So now that we know what the brain is and is not, let's focus on the mind. I believe it is crucial that you get to know your mind.

The following is a list of some important aspects and questions I want you to consider in getting to know <u>your mind</u>:

Three Aspects

- It is God created!
- It is God designed!
- It's a spiritual receiver and transmitter!

Seven Questions

- What is it?
- Where is it?
- How does it work?
- How do you best use it?
- What is the role of your mind in answered prayer?
- How do you renew your mind?
- How can you employ your subconscious mind?

As we proceed, these three aspects will be supported by BCV (book, chapter, and verse), and the seven questions will be answered.

CHAPTER 3:

Getting To Know Your Mind Through Scriptures

Your mind is designed and created by God! Before we get into several scriptures that I believe will be extremely enlightening, ponder these four points:

1. The mind is the first and primary part of the soul, which is comprised of these three components: mind, will, and emotions.

> Many are the plans in a person's heart, but it is the LORD's purpose that prevails.
> —Proverbs 19:21 NIV

> The mind of man plans his way, but the LORD directs his steps.
> —Proverbs. 16:9 NASB

2. God designed the mind of man to function and operate in a very specific manner. It is a design of perfection, for perfection, by perfection.

3. The God-created mind is the very foundation of what is considered the "law of the mind." Interestingly, the law of the mind is supported and validated by science. From the spiritual perspective, this fact is rather unusual. Typically, science tends to focus on disproving spiritual influences, but in the case of the mind, science has substantiated what is referred to as the law of the mind![1] This, of course, is an extremely wide and deep topic that we are not going to try and exhaust in our study here. But we will drill deep enough to lay the foundation that God is revealing to us today.
4. Scriptures clearly address the mind of man as a component with the leading role in God's plan, will, and purpose for our lives.

We will get to know the mind by beginning with scriptures right from the Word of God. There are two types of the mind. The spiritual mind and the carnal mind. The carnal mind operates to the law of sin and death. The spiritual mind operates to the law of spirit and life. When the carnal mind is renewed by the Word of God, it is transformed into a spiritual mind. A mind transformation takes place as described in scripture.

> Don't copy the behavior and customs of this world, but let God transform you into a new person by changing the way you think. Then you will learn to know God's will for you, which is good and pleasing and perfect.
> —Romans 12:2 NLT

> For in my inner being I delight in God's law; but I see another law at work in me, waging war against the law of my mind and making me a prisoner of the law of sin at work within me. Thanks be to God, who de-

livers me through Jesus Christ our Lord! . . . So then, I myself in my mind am a slave to God's law, but in my sinful nature a slave to the law of sin.
—Romans 7:22-23, 25 NIV

Those who live according to the flesh have their minds set on what the flesh desires; but those who live in accordance with the Spirit have their minds set on what the Spirit desires. The mind governed by the flesh is death, but the mind governed by the Spirit is life and peace. The mind governed by the flesh is hostile to God; it does not submit to God's law, nor can it do so. Those who are in the realm of the flesh cannot please God.
—Romans 8:5-8

And He who searches our hearts knows the mind of the Spirit, because the Spirit intercedes for God's people in accordance with the will of God.
—Romans 8:27

It is the mind of the Spirit that connects the Saints to the will of God. It is the spirit of the mind that transforms the Saints as God wills. The mind of the Spirit is the Mind of God, which is also the mind of Christ! The Mind of God is the only Universal Mind.

So, just to clarify . . . it is the mind of the Spirit that connects, and it is the spirit of the mind that transforms. Notice that the mind of the Spirit begins with a big "S" and the spirit of your mind begins with a small "s." The big "S" is God's Spirit and the small "s" is your spirit.

Who has known the mind of the Lord?
—Romans 11:34a NIV

> For who can know the Lord's thoughts? Who knows enough to give Him advice?
> —Romans 11:34 NLT

When we are born again, we receive the mind of Christ as a part of our salvation. First Corinthians confirms that we have the mind of Christ.

> For, "Who can know the Lord's thoughts? Who knows enough to teach Him?" But we understand these things, for we have the mind of Christ.
> —1 Corinthians 2:16

The Lord instructs us through the mind of Christ, which we possess. Ephesians 4:23 tells us that we can renew the thoughts and attitudes of our mind which was designed and created by God.

> And be renewed in the Spirit of your mind.
> —Ephesians 4:23 KJV

The New Living Translation states it in a different way:

> Instead, let the Spirit renew your thoughts and attitudes.
> —Ephesians 4:23 NLT

> God is saying to you, "Let this mind be in you which was also in Christ Jesus."
> —Philippians 2:5 NKJV

Philippians 4:7 promises us peace of mind. That is God's design, and we can experience God's peace, which transcends all understanding and guards our hearts and minds in Christ Jesus. God also instructs us to set our minds on things above, not on things on the earth. The way to live above the cares of this world or the cares on earth, is to set your mind on things above the earth (see Colossians 3:2).

You have to *choose* to set your mind. It is a conscious choice! If you don't set your mind on purpose, then it will get set by default. You definitely don't want to be double-minded as in James 1:8, that is, unstable in all your ways. And being double-minded, you cannot expect to receive anything from the Lord. That includes your prayers, affirmations, and declarations going unanswered. The mind you want to have is the mind God has given you. And that is a sound mind.

> For God hath not given us a spirit of fear; but of power, and of love, and of a sound mind.
> —2 Timothy 1:7 KJV

You have been given a mind mighty in the Spirit of God with divine power to destroy strongholds; cast down arguments, imaginations, and every lofty thing raised up against the knowledge of God; and taking every thought captive to make it obey Christ. That is the kind of mind you want to have. It is the mind of a victor, not a victim.

CHAPTER 4:

One Mind

God's desire is that we not have one mind but be of one mind . . . the same mind. The same mind as what?

Let's keep going to see.

Romans 15:6 (NIV) addresses the Church being of <u>one mind</u>: "so that with one mind and one voice you may glorify the God and Father of our Lord Jesus Christ."

In 1 Corinthians 1:10 (NKJV), we see that we are to be <u>perfectly joined together in the same mind</u>, which I refer to as the "collective mind."

In 2 Corinthians 13:11, we are told again to be of one mind.

Philippians says to be of <u>one spirit</u>, with <u>one mind</u>:

> Only conduct yourselves in a manner worthy of the gospel of Christ, so that whether I come and see you or remain absent, I will hear of you that you are standing firm in <u>one spirit</u>, with <u>one mind</u> striving together for the faith of the gospel.
> —Philippians 1:27 NASB

Philippians also speaks to the unity of being of one mind:

> [T]hen make my joy complete by being like-minded, having the same love, being one in spirit and of one mind. —Philippians 2:2

And in Peter, we are reminded once again:

> Finally, be ye of one mind.
> —1 Peter 3:8 KJV

The only way we, the Church, can be of the same mind or be one mind is to be renewed in the spirit of your mind. It is the Spirit of God that is the unity factor for us being of one mind or the same mind. You see, our hearts and minds *belong* to God:

> For this is the covenant that I will make with the house of Israel after those days, says the Lord: I will put My laws in their mind and write them on their hearts; and I will be their God, and they shall be My people.
> —Hebrews 8:10 NKJV

The above verse sets the stage for the last scripture that we will use to confirm that we are "one mind," and it leaves zero doubt that your mind and your heart is your direct link to God, your Heavenly Father!

The following verse is a basic duplicate of Hebrews 8:10, and I believe God said it twice to make sure we got it.

> This is the covenant that I will make with them after those days, says the Lord: I will put My laws into their hearts, and in their minds will I write them.
> —Hebrews 10:16

Our hearts and minds belong to God by covenant. God is connected to man through the heart and the mind of man.

There is only *one mind*!! The mind of God, which is the one Universal Intelligence. The mind of God is the master mind, or better yet, the *Master's* mind! God created us in His image and gave us His mind. Therefore, as a born-again believer, you are directly connected to God through your mind.

> For who has known the mind and purpose of the Lord, so as to instruct Him? But we have the mind of Christ [to be guided by His thoughts and purposes].
> —1 Corinthians 2:16 AMP

God created the mind, and the God designed and created mind of man has a defined purpose that we, as Christians, have not fully understood nor utilized. God wants us to better understand the mind, its role in our daily lives, and its power.

There are many non-Christians that have a better understanding and utilization of their mind than born-again believers. Knowledge and understanding of how the mind works is the key to the divine application of its power. So we are going to drive our knowledge and understanding to a higher level now that we have established our connectivity to the mind of God.

There are two types of mind—the carnal and the spiritual:

> For to be carnally minded is death; but to be spiritually minded is life and peace. Because the carnal mind is enmity against God: for it is not subject to the law of God, neither indeed can be.
> —Romans 8:6-7 KJV

Enmity is defined as "the state or feeling of being actively opposed or hostile to someone or something."[1]

The carnal mind is transformable. It can be transformed into a spiritual mind.

Ephesians 4:23 speaks to a transformation by the renewal of your mind, as it says, "and be renewed in the spirit of your mind."

Romans also encourages us to "be transformed by the renewing of your mind":

> I beseech you therefore, brethren, by the mercies of God, that you present your bodies a living sacrifice, holy, acceptable to God, which is your reasonable service. And do not be conformed to this world, but be transformed by the renewing of your mind, that you may prove what is that good and acceptable and perfect will of God.
> —Romans 12:1-2 NKJV

Philippians tells us that our hearts and minds are guarded by the peace of God. God wants you to have peace of mind and peace in your heart.

> And the peace of God, which surpasses all understanding, will guard your hearts and minds through Christ Jesus.
> —Philippians 4:7

CHAPTER 5:

The Relationship Between Faith and the Mind

What is faith? By definition, faith is complete trust, confidence, or belief in someone or something; a strong belief in God.[1] According to Hebrews 11:1 (KJV), "Now faith is the substance of things hoped for, the evidence of things not seen." Faith is simply trusting in something you cannot explicitly prove.

FAITH could also be an acronym for **F**ull **A**ssurance **I**n **T**rusting **H**im *or* **F**antastic **A**dventure **I**n **T**rusting **H**im.

Faith cometh by hearing and hearing by the word of God. How does this tie in or relate to the mind? The subconscious mind is where faith resides. It's where your belief system exists and operates. What you believe and trust in is within your subconscious mind. So if faith cometh by hearing and hearing by the word of God, then we need to feed, program, and calibrate our beliefs with the Word of God, and faith will develop and grow. You cannot stop it. Faith cometh . . . into your *subconscious* mind!

Faith, by definition, is:

1. A firm belief in what another states, affirms, or testifies, simply on the ground of his truth or veracity; especially (as distinguished from mere belief), practical dependence on a person, statement, or thing as trustworthy; trust; as, *faith* in a friend (as sincere and true), *faith* in his advice (as wise and good), *faith* in his efforts (as likely to be efficacious).

2. Specifically, in theology, the assent of the mind or understanding to the truth of what God has revealed; belief in the testimony of God as contained in the scriptures; a divinely wrought, loving, and hearty reliance upon God and His promise of salvation through Christ: sometimes called justifying or saving faith; as, we are saved through faith; more widely, operative belief in the truths of religion; as, a serene and blessed faith.[2]

These definitions of faith contain two aspects: intellectual assent and trust. Intellectual assent is believing something is true. Trust is actually relying on the fact that the something you believe is true.

I remember this story about a little boy who was playing one day and fell into an old well. He was unhurt but could not climb up out of the well because of the loose dirt in the walls of the well. A farmer wondering by heard the little boy's shouts for help. This farmer was a big, strong, muscular man of tall stature. The farmer told the little boy that he would go get a rope and come back to lift him out of the well. The little boy stopped the farmer and asked him to go get his father instead to bring a rope. The little boy told the farmer which field his father was plowing in.

The farmer rushed to get the little boy's father and brought him back, showing him where his son was trapped in the well. The boy's father lowered the rope into the well and pulled his son up out of the well. Now, the boy's father was a short, thin man, not very strong-looking.

After the little boy was safely out of the well, the big, strong farmer asked him why he didn't just let him lift him out of the well. The farmer said, "I am much bigger and stronger than your father, and we could have saved a lot of time if I had just pulled you up out of the well."

The little boy, standing next to his father, looked up at the farmer and said, "You see, sir, this is my daddy! I knew he would never let go of the rope, no matter what."

You see, we are talking about the two aspects of faith, and this short story demonstrates trust. The little boy trusted in his daddy and relied on the fact that he would never let go of the rope. The foundation of this little boy's trust was his relationship with his daddy.

A chair is often used to help illustrate the two aspects of faith: intellectual assent and trust. Intellectual assent is recognizing that a chair is a piece of furniture and agreeing that it is designed to support a person who sits in it. Trust is actually physically sitting in the chair.

Understanding these two aspects of faith is crucial. Many people believe certain facts about Jesus Christ. Many people will intellectually agree with the facts that are written in the Bible about Jesus. But knowing those facts to be true is not what the Bible means in regard to "faith." The biblical definition of faith requires intellectual assent to the facts, believing the facts are true, *and* trusting in the truth.

Intellectual assent to the facts requires no physical action. Intellectual assent takes place in the conscious mind. Trust in the facts requires physical action, like sitting in the chair. Trust takes place in the subconscious mind or the heart. You will see later on that these two occupy the same space.

When you sit in a chair, you don't think about it real long and hard. You automatically sit down in the chair, unless you can physically see that the chair may be questionable as to its ability to support you. Faith is important because without faith, it is impossible to please God (Hebrews 11:6). Faith without works (corresponding action) is dead, useless, and fruitless. Therefore, belief or intellectual assent in the conscious mind must connect to and work with trust in the subconscious mind to produce faith. That is how faith to move mountains is developed. And that faith is activated by your "saying." It is the words you speak that have the power to activate faith. Check out the following scripture:

> And Jesus, replying, said to them, "Have faith in God [constantly]. Truly I tell you, whoever says to this mountain, Be lifted up and thrown into the sea! and does not doubt at all in his heart but believes that what he says will take place, it will be done for him. For this reason I am telling you, whatever you ask for in prayer, believe (trust and be confident) that it is granted to you, you will [get it]."
> —Mark 11:22-24 AMPC

I submit to you that the mind, the heart, and the mouth operate together synergistically in producing more power collectively than any one of them individually or the sum of all three. Faith in your heart will work with doubt in your head.

But faith will not work with doubt in your heart. Doubt in your heart will cancel faith.

It is the words you speak that have the power to activate faith.

In Matthew, we see where Peter asked Jesus to explain a parable that He spoke. So Jesus said,

> Are you also still without understanding? Do you not yet understand that whatever enters the mouth goes into the stomach and is eliminated? But those things which proceed out of the mouth come from the heart, and they defile a man. For out of the heart proceed evil thoughts, murders, adulteries, fornications, thefts, false witness, and blasphemies. These are the things which defile a man.
> —Matthew 15:15-20 NKJV

Notice that most all of the things that Jesus said that make a person unclean are physical activities. There is only one that is not physical but produces the same results, and that is your thoughts.

CHAPTER 6:

The Integration of Heart and Mind

The heart is most often thought of as

> the organ in the human body which by its motion keeps the blood in circulation—consequently, the seat of life. It is a common thought with mankind that the heart is the seat of all human affections and passions as well as that of life. The ancients, particularly the Jews, also had the idea that the intellect resided in the heart, and when references to it occur in the Bible, the reader must not lose sight of this fact.[1]

Anytime you read scripture that refers to the heart, it includes the mind. And anytime you read scripture that refers to the mind, it includes the heart.

I am going to make a statement that could create a defining moment. And in an effort to increase understanding for some, here is the definition of a "defining moment": A defining moment is that point in time when you experience something that fundamentally changes you and has a transformative effect on your perceptions and behaviors.[2]

Now, this is the statement: I believe that <u>the heart and mind are homogenous</u>. So what does that mean?

The first definition of "homogeneous" is "of the same kind; alike."[3]

Synonyms include similar, comparable, equivalent, like, parallel, matching, kindred, related, congruent.[4]

The second definition of "homogeneous" is "composed of parts or elements that are all of the same kind."[5]

Synonyms of homogeneous include <u>uniform</u>, <u>identical</u>, unvarying, similar, alike.[6]

Throughout scripture, God refers to the heart and mind as homogeneous.

Here is an interesting question. Are thoughts in our heart or in our mind? We find the answer in Proverbs 23:7 that says, "For as he thinks in his heart, so is he." The heart is a contributing component of the thought process. It plays a key role in <u>how</u> you think. Where do thoughts really occur?

Another scripture that addresses that question is in Luke:

> Jesus knew what they were thinking and asked, "Why are you thinking these things in your hearts?"
> —Luke 5:22 NIV

In Job, we read:

> Who has put wisdom in the mind? Or who has given understanding to the heart?
> —Job 38:36 NKJV

The three-fold cord of intellect is wisdom, knowledge, and understanding. It's all in the mind.

According to Proverbs, we can see how God works with and through us:

> A man's mind plans his way, but the Lord directs his steps and makes them sure.
> —Proverbs 16:9 AMPC

A different version of the same scripture reads:

> A man's heart plans his way: but the Lord directs his steps.
> —Proverbs 16:9 NKJV

Both versions are accurate, as we will establish and demonstrate shortly. The heart and the mind occupy the same space and work together so closely that it is difficult to distinguish the difference. A person makes plans with their conscious mind, but God establishes their steps through their subconscious mind. This is the work of the Divine Infinite Intelligence within the subconscious mind . . . being led by the Holy Spirit!

It is written:

> The spirit of man [that factor in human personality which proceeds immediately from God] is the lamp of the Lord, searching all his innermost parts.
> —Proverbs 20:27 AMPC

Another relevant verse is in Corinthians:

> For what person perceives (knows and understands) what passes through a man's thoughts except the man's own spirit within him? Just so no one discerns (comes to know and comprehend) the thoughts of God except the Spirit of God.
> —1 Corinthians 2:11

And a part of Hebrews 4:12 (KJV) also connects thoughts and the heart. It says that the Word of God is a discerner of the thoughts and intents of the heart.

Now, the last reference I want to make to establish the connection between man's mind and heart is found in Jeremiah:

> I the LORD search the heart and examine the mind,
> to reward each person according to their conduct,
> according to what their deeds deserve.
> —Jeremiah 17:10 NIV

My question here is, what conduct have you displayed before the Lord God and what deserving deeds have you performed to qualify for His reward?

The Heart

Let's examine the relationship of both the heart and mind by considering multiple definitions. I believe this will help us to focus more clearly on what God means when He addresses the terms "heart" and "mind" so many times in His Word.

The English language is so complex that we have to deal with different ways of spelling the same word, different pronunciations of the same word, and different meanings of the same word. For example, in our study, let's consider the word "heart." There are multiple definitions and multiple uses of the word "heart" in different situations, for different purposes, and on different occasions. But let's zero in on the spiritual nature and meaning of the word "heart," instead of the physical nature and meaning of the heart.

Heart (hart) noun

1. The central organ of the vascular system of animals; a hollow muscular structure which maintains the circulation of the blood by alternate contraction (systole) and dilatation (diastole).
2. The seat of the affections and passions as distinguished from the intellect and will; the emotional nature; feelings; intentions and personality as, his heart is better than his head. Or charge it to the head and not the *heart.**
3. Sometimes, the intellect and will, or even the entire personality considered capable of being moved or influenced; as in, he loves with all his heart.
4. Susceptibility to emotion; predominant sensibility as distinguished from intellect; tenderness; love; as in, the girl is all *heart.*
5. Capacity for endurance or enjoyment; courage; resolution; spirit; as in, take *heart.*
6. The breast regarded as the seat of the heart or affections; as in, clasped to one's *heart.*
7. The chief central, or vital part of interest; middle or central portion; the core; inner significances; as in, let us go to the *heart* of the matter.
8. A bold or high-spirited man; as in, brave *heart.*
9. One of various things shaped like a heart or located centrally in a manner analogous to a heart; specifically, a red heart-shaped figure or spot on a playing card; any card bearing such figures; in the plural, the suit as marked; also a cherry of one of many varieties having the shape

of a heart; or, in botany, the inner part or core of a tree or plant.

10. A term of endearment, praise, or encouragement; as in, be of cheer, my *heart*.[7]

As it is easy to see, there are many uses of the term "heart." Here is a partial list of some typical uses of the term:

- After One's Own Heart—Suiting one perfectly; conforming to one's ideas; to one's taste; as, a man after one's own heart. (David was a man after God's own heart.)
- At Heart—At the center or bottom; essentially; substantially; in fact.
- By Heart—By rote (mechanical or habitual repetition) so as to memorize perfectly: said of recitations. (Reciting by heart.)
- From One's Heart—With all sincerity.
- To Have at Heart—To cherish someone or something; be concerned for someone or something earnestly.
- To Have One's Heart in One's Mouth or Throat—To be excessively excited or frightened.
- To Have the Heart—To have the necessary will (to do something).
- To Wear One's Heart on One's Sleeve—To show one's feelings plainly.
- With All One's Heart—Intensely; thoroughly; completely; wholly. (Love the Lord your God with all your heart.)

The best short and sweet definition I found for the term "heart" is as follows: Heart—The supposed seat of the intellect, soul (mind, will, and emotions), etc.[8]

In the Greek, the word "heart" is defined in a way that coincides and further clarifies the significates already established in English. I believe that the combination of Greek and English definitions really helps us to see what God had in mind (pun intended) when He created man.

The Greek word for "heart" is *kardia* (kar-dee'-ah), and definitions for the heart include:

- Denotes the center of all physical and spiritual life
- The center and seat of spiritual life
    - The soul or mind, as it is the fountain and seat of the thoughts, passions, desires, appetites, affections, purposes, endeavors, sincerity
    - Of the understanding, the faculty and seat of the intelligence
    - Of the will and character
    - Of the soul so far as it is affected and stirred in a bad way or good, or of the soul as the seat of sensibilities, affections, emotions, desires, appetites, passions, sincerity[9]

Now to take the definition of "heart" one step further: let's consider the word in Hebrew.

The Hebrew word for "heart" is *leb* (lebe, pronounced lev).[10] In biblical Hebrew, the heart is where we feel feelings and think thoughts. The heart is also where we make choices. So the concept of "the heart" is best understood as the "inner person"—the seat of our mind (thoughts), emotions (feelings), and will (intentions).

Though personal studies, I have determined that to the ancient Hebrews, the heart was the mind and the thoughts. When Deuteronomy 6:5 tells us to love the Lord our God with all our heart, with all our soul, and with all our strength, it is not speaking of or referring to an emotional love but to keep our minds and our thoughts fixed on Him.

Hebrew definitions include but are not limited to inner man, mind, will, heart, and understanding.[11]

According to Strong's definitions, the heart is also used (figuratively) very widely for the feelings, the will, and even the intellect.[12]

As you can see, we can hardly talk about the heart without it referring to the mind, and we can hardly talk about the mind without including the heart. The heart and the mind overlap and are inseparable. They occupy the same space and form a perfect union.

I believe we can all agree that we think in our mind, but the heart also thinks.

Here are four scriptures that confirm the heart's spiritual-intellectual functions:

> But Jesus, knowing their thoughts, said, "Why do you think evil in your hearts?"
> —Matthew 9:4 ESV

> Immediately Jesus knew in his spirit that this was what they were thinking in their hearts, and He said to them, "Why are you thinking these things?
> —Mark 2:8 NIV

The heart does remember and meditate:

> I call to remembrance my song in the night; with my heart I meditate and my spirit searches diligently.
> —Psalm 77:6 AMPC

All who heard the shepherds' story were astonished, but Mary kept all these things in her heart and thought about them often.
—Luke 2:18–19 NLT

The Mind

Mind (noun)

1. An abstract, collective term for all forms of conscious intelligence, or for the subject of all conscious states; especially, the activity or faculty of knowing.
2. Any mental state or activity; any state or act of the intellect; consciousness; contemplation; consideration; thought; opinion; conclusion; the state or act of remembering; memory; recollection; as, to bear in mind; any state or act of the feelings; mood; inclination; desire; liking; disposition or mental tendency; as, a cheerful mind; a man of strange mind; any state or act of will; choice; decision; purpose; as, to make up one's mind.
3. The power of cognition or thought.
4. <u>The spirit or intelligence pervading the universe</u>: opposed to matter.*
5. The intellect or reason in its normal condition; sanity.
6. A person regarded chiefly as a <u>unity of mental powers</u>: sometimes used <u>collectively</u>.[13]

Synonyms (noun) Explained

Consciousness, instinct, intellect, intelligence, reason, sense, soul, spirit, thought, understanding are common synonyms for the mind.[14] *Mind* includes all the powers of sentient being apart from the physical factors in bodily faculties and activities; in a limited sense, mind is nearly synonymous with intellect but includes disposition, or the tendency toward action, as appears in the phrase "to have a mind to work" (see Nehemiah 4:6). The intellect is that assemblage of faculties which is concerned with knowledge, as distinguished from emotion and volition. Understanding is chiefly used of the reasoning powers: the understanding is distinguished by many philosophers from reason in that reason is the faculty of the high cognitions or a priority truth. Thought, the act, process, or power of thinking, is often used to denote the thinking faculty, and especially the reason. The instinct of animals is held to be of the same nature as the intellect of man, but inferior and limited; yet the apparent difference is very great. Human instincts denote tendencies independent of reasoning or instruction. Sense is used as denoting clear mental action, good judgment, acumen; as, he is a man of sense, or he showed good sense. Consciousness includes all that a sentient being perceives, knows, thinks, or feels, from *whatever source.*

Compare the Definitions of Mind (Above) to Soul (Below)

Soul (noun)

1. In present general acceptation, the incorporeal nature of man, or principle of mental and spiritual life; the thinking, willing nature.
2. The essence, heart, or animating principle of anything.
3. The vital principle together with mental power.

4. The moral and emotional nature as distinguished from the more purely intellectual and scientific powers and operations.[15]

Synonyms of the word "soul" include mind and spirit.[16] The soul includes the intellect, sensibilities, and will; beyond what is expressed by the word "mind," the soul denotes especially the moral, the immortal nature; we say of a dead body, the soul (not the mind) has fled. Spirit is used especially in contradistinction from matter; it may, in many cases, be substituted for soul, but soul has commonly a fuller and more determinate meaning. (Compare to "mind.")

Compare the Greek and Hebrew Definitions for "Mind" and "Soul"

So let's look at the Greek and Hebrew definitions of "mind" and "soul." There is a wide variation in interpretations across the English, Greek and Hebrew definitions of these words.

*The Greek word for "mind" is *nous* (nooce).[17] Short definitions include:

- The mind (divine or human), intellect, understanding, thought, feeling, or will

Some longer definitions include faculties of perceiving and understanding, the intellectual faculty, the capacity for spiritual truth, and the faculty of perceiving divine things.[18]

*The Hebrew word for "mind" is *leb* (labe). The short definition includes:

- <u>Heart</u>
- Inner man, mind, will, heart[19]

Now when we compare the Greek and Hebrew definitions of the word "heart," we see an undeniable similarity with the word "mind."

The Greek word for "heart" is *kardia* (kar-dee'-ah). Short definitions include:

- The heart, inner life, intention
- The heart; mind, character, inner self, will, intention, center[20]

Note: Heart (*kardia*) is mentioned over eight hundred times in scripture, but never referring to the literal physical pump that drives the circulation of blood in the body.[21]

- Universally denotes the seat and center of all physical and spiritual life
- The center and seat of spiritual life, "the soul or mind, <u>as it is the foundation and seat of the thoughts</u>, passions, desires, appetites, affections, purposes, endeavors (so in English, heart, inner man, etc.)[22]

Other definitions of "heart" include understanding, intelligence, of the will and character, and of the soul so far as it is affected and stirred in a bad way or good, or of the soul as the seat of the sensibilities, affections, emotions, desires, appetites, and passions.[23]

*The Hebrew word for "heart" is leb (labe). It is very interesting to see that the Hebrew word for "heart" and "mind" are the same . . . leb (labe). Short definitions for "heart" include:

- Inner man, mind, will, heart[24]

Compare the asterisks (*) for mind and heart above!

Note that to the ancient Hebrews, the heart was the mind, the thoughts: (lev or levav)—the center of human thought and spiritual life.[25]

Now, to put all of the English, Hebrew, and Greek definitions into the proper perspective, please also note that the Bible was originally written mainly in Hebrew. The very first translation of the Hebrew Bible was into Greek. So the foundation was basically biblical Hebrew, sometimes called Classical Hebrew.

The Soul

When writing about the soul, the Bible writers used the Hebrew word *ne'phesh* or the Greek word *psy-khe'*. These two words occur well over eight hundred times in the scriptures.[26] Anything that is mentioned or addressed that many times must be of primary importance.

The Greek word for "soul" is *psuche'* (psoo-khay'). Short definitions include:

- The soul, life, self, breath
- The vital breath, breath of life
- The human soul
- The soul as the seat of affections and will
- The self
- A human person, an individual

Note: "to breathe, blow" which is the root of the English words "psyche," and "psychology"—Soul (psyche): a person's distinct identity (unique personhood), i.e., individual personality.[27]

The soul is the direct aftermath of God breathing (blowing) His gift of life into a person, making them an ensouled being. They become a host for the One that is the Breath of Life . . . God. The Breath of Life is the Spirit of God. This supports the statement that God is as close to us as the air we breathe.[28]

The Hebrew word for "soul" is nephesh (neh'fesh). Here's a short definition:

- A soul, living being, life, self, person, desire, passion, appetite, emotion[29]

I originally did not plan to include information on the soul, but I was moved and inspired to do so because it really follows so closely to the definitions of heart and mind previously covered. I believed it would help you to more completely understand how God designed and intended for the mind to work. It is easy to see the similarity and crossover among the definitions of heart, mind, and soul. There is a divine-designed synergy of these three that is powerful and much like a three-fold cord. It is very important to understand how God purposefully created the three parts of your spiritual-intellectual being, in His likeness, before we dive into how the mind works. And there is only one source that we want to focus on for learning how the mind works. That one source is God, who is *Universal Intelligence.* Understanding the relationship between God and your mind will enable and empower you to establish and employ the work of your Divine Mind.

In the book of John, Jesus states our connection to Him and our dependence on Him. He said,

> Abide in Me, and I in you. As the branch cannot bear fruit of itself, unless it abides in the vine, neither can you, unless you abide in Me. I am the vine, you are

> the branches. He who abides in Me, and I in him, bears much fruit; for without Me you can do nothing. If anyone does not abide in me, he is cast out as a branch and is withered; and they gather them and throw them into the fire and they are burned. If you abide in Me, and My words abide in you, you will ask what you desire, and it shall be done for you. By this My Father is glorified, that you bear much fruit; so you will be My disciples.
>
> —John 15:4—8 NKJV

Again, Jesus said, "Abide in Me and I [will abide] in you." To abide means to remain; dwell; inhabit; reside; stay. Now, God is spirit. So where in you does He abide, as a spirit? It is within your mind! The spirit of God actually abides in you within your subconscious mind. Your subconscious mind is your switchboard for two-way communication with God. So it is extremely important to know and understand how the mind, that God created in you, works!

God wants you to know the truth about the science of the mind and the spirit of the mind. These two, believe it or not, work together to facilitate answered prayer. With that said, let's think back to 1 Thessalonians 5:23 where it is written and scripturally validated that man is a spirit, he has a soul (mind, will, and emotions), and he lives in a body. All three parts of man work together (spirit, soul, and body). Our focus from this point forward is going to be the mind of man and how it works. That is important because the more you understand about how your mind works, the better you will be able to employ your mind.

As we have discussed and acknowledged earlier in 1 Corinthians 2:16, we have the mind of Christ. As born-again believers and followers of Christ, our soul is influenced by the Lord. May I remind you that your soul is made up of your mind, your will, and your emotions? Reread the verse below, and consider the role of your soul:

> But we have the mind of Christ (the Messiah) and do <u>hold the thoughts (feelings and purposes) of His heart</u>.
> —1 Corinthians 2:16b AMPC

According to this verse, the mind of Christ that we have is what connects us to the thoughts, feelings, and purposes of His heart. As you look a little closer at this verse, you will see that your soul is involved. Because thoughts represent your mind, purposes represent your will, and feelings represent your emotions. I believe the most powerful component of the soul is the mind, which manages our thoughts. The act of thinking produces thoughts. Thinking is critical, because as scripture says,

> For as he thinks in his heart, so is he.
> —Proverbs 23:7 NKJV

The way you think determines who, what, and how you will be. Your life will follow the thoughts in your conscious mind, but your life will <u>become</u> the thoughts of your subconscious mind. In Romans 8:5–6, Paul is saying that your life is a result of how you set your mind. How you live your life is governed by your mindset. And your mindset is established by your words. <u>Your declaration determines the trajectory of your destiny</u>.

So really, where does thinking take place? As a man thinks where? In his heart. Wait a minute. We think in our minds.

Is your mind in your heart, or is your heart in your mind? I submit to you that your heart and your mind are tightly intertwined. Now we are not talking about the physical heart . . . the organ that pumps blood throughout your body. We are talking about the heart of your spirit (spiritual heart), not the physical heart of your body.

So what things should you be thinking? Things that develop you into who, what, and how you want to be or how you want things to be in your life. Here are three scriptures that speak to this matter of right thinking and its benefits:

> And now, dear brothers and sisters, one final thing. Fix your thoughts on what is true, and honorable, and right, and pure, and lovely, and admirable. Think about things that are excellent and worthy of praise.
> —Philippians 4:8 NLT

> This Book of the Law shall not depart out of your mouth, but you shall mediate on it day and night, that you may observe and do according to all that is written in it. For then you shall make your way prosperous, and then you shall deal wisely and have good success.
> —Joshua 1:8 AMPC

> But you shall [earnestly] remember the Lord your God, for it is He who gives you power to get wealth, that He may establish His covenant which He swore to your fathers, as it is this day.
> —Deuteronomy 8:18

In the above verse in Deuteronomy, God is addressing a covenant of increase and prosperity.

God also wants us to take great pleasure in Him so He can deliver great pleasures to us . . . as we see in the following verse:

> Take delight in the Lord, and He will give you the desires of your heart.
> —Psalm 37:4 NIV

Taking delight in the Lord is done through your mind and heart. Delight begins with your thoughts and comes out of your mouth. Remember, out of the abundance of the heart, the mouth speaks. Let your soul delight in the Lord and prepare to receive the desires of your heart. The truth is, we have two hearts. We have a physical heart and a spiritual heart. That does not make us freaks or sci-fi aliens. It makes us God's spiritual beings. That is the way He created us on purpose. When you take delight in the Lord, the Lord takes delight in you and his delight is to bless you.

God also gives a warning in Deuteronomy that supports the truth that thoughts are in your heart:

> Beware that there be not a thought in thy wicked heart, saying, . . .
> —Deuteronomy 15:9(a) KJV

> Beware lest there be a wicked thought in your heart, saying, . . .
> —Deuteronomy 15:9(a) NKJV

Please notice that both, a thought and your heart, have the potential to be wicked. This demonstrates mutual influence between a thought and your heart. So it is always wise to guard your heart. King Solomon said it best: "Above all else, guard your heart, for it is the wellspring of life" (see Proverbs 4:23). The best way to guard your heart is through your mind. Your mind is like an antivirus software for your heart. Philippians 4:7 tells us that the peace of God, which surpasses all understanding, will guard your heart and mind.

CHAPTER 7:

The Integration of Mind and Mouth

God gives you the power to attain wealth (see Deuteronomy 8:18), but a lot of Christians have not gotten wealthy. God has already laid up the wealth of the wicked for the righteous. It is laid up, but you have to go get it. How do you get it? Where do you go to get it? And where is that power He speaks of to get wealth?

The power to get wealth is in your mind and your mouth. If Jesus can speak money into the mouth of a fish, surely He can speak it into your mouth. Better yet, you can speak in into your life. God said that life and death, blessing and cursing, are in the power of the tongue. Also, abundance and lack, peace and conflict. The thoughts in your mind and the words you speak have tremendous *power*! Creative power!!

When the thoughts of your mind, the meditation of your heart, and the words of your mouth align with the Word and Spirit of God, you will release creative power in your life.

How Powerful Is Your Declaration?

The words "and God said" are found in the book of Genesis, chapter 1, several times. You can also say! And you can have whatever you say. But you must have the conviction to believe and not doubt. Let's look at the words of Jesus in the following:

> So Jesus answered and said to them, "Have faith in God. For assuredly, I say to you, whoever says to this mountain, 'Be removed and be cast into the sea,' and does not doubt in his heart, but believes that those things he says will be done, he will have whatever he says. Therefore I say to you, whatever things you ask when you pray, believe that you receive them, and you will have them."
> —Mark 11: 22-24 NKJV

There is creative power in your mind, and in your mouth. But when you combine the two and then add the heart . . . *wow*!! Look out. Things will *not* stay the same.

CHAPTER 8:

The Science of Mind

So far we have covered

- The God-created mind is a part of your soul.
- The mind is designed by God for His purpose.
- The mind is our source of connection to God.
- We have the same mind . . . the mind of Christ.

Now let's go a little wider and deeper into understanding the mind of man. We will cover various aspects of the mind, such as

* What it is
* How it works
* Its role
* How it gets programmed

Colossians 3:2 says, "<u>Set your mind</u> on things above, not on things on the earth."

How do you set your mind? How do you renew your mind? Both are accomplished by the way you think!

Romans 12:2 (NLT) reads, "Don't copy the behavior and customs of this world, but let God transform you into a new person by changing the way you think. Then you will learn to know God's will for you, which is good and pleasing and perfect."

The Mind—What Is It?

First, let's address what the mind is not. It is not the brain! Mind and brain are not the same. God created the brain in your head, but He also gave us a sound mind (see 2 Timothy 1:7). The brain is physical and the mind is spiritual. The brain is subject to the mind, is a servant of the mind, and is also directed by the mind. That's the way God made us. God/Holy Spirit most often speaks to us through our mind, but it also impacts our brain. Thoughts are in the mind and memories are in the brain. Think about a computer. The mind is like the software and the brain is like the hard drive, and they are connected. They work together very effectively, but with very different functions to guide you through life, much like a GPS in your car.

There is so much fascinating new information about how the brain works: proof and support that is made available through research and technological advancements in science. There is also considerable scientific proof that connects the functions of the brain to thoughts in the mind. Understanding how thoughts affect the brain is supported by current and on-going scientific and medical research.

* * *

Now, as we mentioned earlier, there are two types of mind: the spiritual mind and the carnal (flesh) mind.

> The mind governed by the flesh is death, but the mind governed by the Spirit is life and peace.
> —Romans 8:6 NIV

So what is the mind? The mind is the element of a person that enables them to be aware of the world and their experiences. It enables them to think and to feel. The mind is also the faculty of consciousness and thought. And finally, the mind can be considered a person's intellect.[1]

Now there are actually three parts of the mind.[2] The first two are the conscious mind and the subconscious mind. There is also the unconscious mind. We will discuss the third part of the mind later. But for right now, we will address both the conscious and subconscious, but we shall concentrate our focus on the power of the subconscious mind.

In order to best use the power of your subconscious mind, you must first understand how the subconscious mind works. The subconscious mind is governed by several laws. Learning about these laws will allow you to make the most use of your subconscious mind with the least amount of effort.

Answered Prayers

In James 5:16 (NKJV), it is written, "The effectual fervent prayer of a righteous man avails much." We probably can all agree that prayer is a spiritual activity, however it can also be a scientific activity. Let me explain. Scientific prayer is the creative interaction of the conscious and subconscious parts of the mind that can be scientifically governed for desired results. If you could aim and focus your prayers like a laser beam on a target, it could and would help to increase the probability and frequency of your answered prayers. So, for this reason, you should desire to learn how the conscious and subconscious parts of your mind work together and understand how to apply a few simple techniques to influence and direct your subconscious mind.

What do you believe in? It is not what you believe in that answers a prayer. The answer to prayer comes when your subconscious mind responds to the mental impressions, images or thoughts in your conscious mind. Do not zone out on me now! We are addressing the process of answered prayers, not the source.

We acknowledge the only true source of answered prayers is the Lord God Almighty. The seeds of thought that you sow into your conscious mind will drop down into your subconscious mind and begin to produce that which was sown. In this process, belief is birthed. The Law of Belief can be expressed as a thought that is received and accepted in your mind and in your heart. Answered prayer is the manifestation and realization of your heart's desire. Everyone has desires. We need to gain a knowledge of how our mind works, because that knowledge could enable us to receive the desires of our heart or contribute to our prayers being answered. There is one universal mind that is common to all individual believers . . . it is the mind of Christ:

> Let this mind be in you, which was also in Christ Jesus: Who, being in the form of God, thought it not robbery to be equal with God.
> —Philippians 2:5-6

For who has known the mind of the Lord that he may instruct Him? But we have the mind of Christ.
—1 Corinthians 2:16

To help you grasp the concept of the subconscious mind, let's consider someone learning to ride a motorcycle. The operational functions are similar in nature but different in technique and apparatus from driving a standard transmission car. Everything for operating a motorcycle is different from a car. All controls are located differently. The brakes and clutch are located on the handlebars, along with the throttle control for acceleration, just like the gas pedal in a car. The gear shift for changing gears is operated by foot and not by hand, and the brakes are operated by hand and not by foot. The shift pattern is also different. So as you can see the differences are major between driving a standard transmission car and riding a motorcycle.

So, in the beginning, someone learning to ride a motorcycle must concentrate on and briefly focus on each function in the motorcycle riding process, because of unfamiliarity. And in the beginning, mistakes will be made. They will fail to give it enough gas with the throttle or use the front brakes too forcefully . . . if they remember to apply the hand-operated brakes at all. They will experience stall-outs and jerky pull offs, as well as shifting into the wrong gear and more.

Learning to do all of these things together while keeping the motorcycle upright and balanced, without falling over to the side, is a major adjustment. But with time and experience, it all comes together with efficiency and without conscious thought. It is almost instinctive. This takes place when all the functions in the motorcycle riding process are transferred from the conscious mind to the subconscious mind. When this happens, the conscious mind becomes free to enjoy the pleasure of the riding experience and the open-air view, not to mention the need to watch out for other vehicles in traffic. That's how the subconscious mind works.

The conscious mind handles reasoning and processing the logic of lane changes, speed, passing maneuvers, stopping-distance calculations, and interpretation of other information. The conscious mind also processes pictures/images, written words, and spoken words, along with all the actions performed while we are in a conscious state of being aware, awake, and alert. The subconscious mind, on the other hand, controls bodily functions such as heartbeats, blood pressure, sweating, breathing, salivation, tears, and every other involuntary function of your body.[3]

There is another really simple demonstration of how the subconscious mind works and the role it plays in life and living. I want you to participate in this simple demonstration.

Let's consider the simple act or function of breathing. Now, breathing is one of those involuntary functions of your body that we just listed. Breathing is also taken for granted until we are physically unable to do so. Remember, breathing is controlled, <u>for the most part</u>, by your subconscious mind. And I say for the most part because I want you to right now take control of your breathing by changing and controlling its rhythm, its frequency, and its duration. I want to prove to you, with a demonstration, that breathing is controlled by your subconscious mind.

So begin by slowing down your breathing, for five breaths. Now, speed up your breathing for five breaths. Next, hold your breath for as long as you possibly can . . . go as long as you can without taking another breath. What you will discover is that when it comes time to take another breath, it will be a subconscious decision. Your subconscious mind will not allow you to continue to hold your breath to your detriment. Your subconscious mind will override your conscious effort to continue to hold your breath to the point of harming yourself.

For a time, your conscious mind was controlling your breathing, but when you stopped focusing your conscious mind on the control of each breath, your subconscious mind took control again. This represents one facet of the subconscious mind. But I want you to understand another facet of the subconscious. I want you to see if the following two definitions of different facets of the subconscious mind will align with the two demonstrations we addressed.

Subconscious (adjective): Denoting such phenomena of mental life as are not attended by full consciousness, as the many automatic processes involved in the performance of familiar actions.[4] Such as the example of riding a motorcycle.

Subconscious (noun): That portion of mental activity not directly in the focus of consciousness but capable of being called into consciousness by the proper stimulus. With the proper stimulus, you can program the subconscious mind through your conscious mind. This is a scientific fact and a spiritual truth.[5] And it is extremely powerful!

> And do not be conformed to this world, but be transformed by the renewing of your mind, that you may prove what is that good and acceptable and perfect will of God.
> —Romans 12:2

It is important to understand how to program your subconscious mind and know what program content you should use. My recommendation is to start with scriptures from the Word of God. The information about riding a motorcycle is stored in your subconscious mind as a software program. Think of your mind as a computer and the motorcycle riding information as software that can operate automatically whenever the need arises.

When you learned to ride a bicycle as a young child, with or without training wheels, you have never forgotten how to ride. The core programming of that process has been stored in your subconscious for years, even decades. But if you were to sit on a bicycle today and attempt to ride it, the information and experience from decades ago will automatically upload to meet the demand for your success. The same thing goes for many other activities, goals, desires, emotions, prayers, etc.

By programming your subconscious mind with new information, you are being transformed by the renewing of your mind. The best way to renew/program your mind is by the Word of God.

By programming your subconscious mind with new intel/information, you can change situations or have the desires of your heart. Your subconscious mind operates on autopilot at all times. It is the operating system running in the background 24 hours a day, 7 days a week, and 365 days a year. It never stops! Even when you sleep, it does not stop. It continues to work perpetually.[6]

How The Mind Works

Our mind is not just our conscious thoughts, our reasoning, or our intellect, but a holistic system that is complex and complicated. It begins with the Holy Spirit for a Divine Mind, or an unholy spirit for a devious mind. And they both end with our actions and choices, with a lot of stuff in between. This can be considered a prelude to understanding how the mind works, especially the subconscious mind, which will lead into our primary focus on the unconscious mind.

The most powerful, precious, and valuable part of you is your mind. Your greatest treasure is your subconscious mind. It holds the secrets to all your failures and successes in life. The subconscious mind is governed by several scientific and spiritual laws. Learning about these laws will prepare and empower you to apply these laws to maximize the power of your subconscious mind with minimum time, energy, or effort.

We are going to briefly highlight some of these laws. Learning how to unleash the divine power of your subconscious mind will potentially change your life. I say potentially change your life because just learning something or gaining knowledge about something has no power to change anything. We have all heard the statement that "knowledge is power," but that is not true. Knowledge is not power, knowledge is *potential* . . . applied knowledge is power!

The power of the subconscious mind is a hidden power that most people never truly and fully discover in their lifetime. The truth is that no one needs to acquire this power, simply because it already exist within each one of us. We just need to learn how to engage it and employ it. Think about a set of mechanical gears that are designed to best work together when they are engaged with each other. The power of the gear assembly only works when they are engaged. You need to understand how the subconscious mind works so you can apply its power in any area of your life. If you don't understand how the subconscious mind works, then you will be unable to employ it and make it work for you.

Divine Intelligence through your subconscious mind can provide whatever you need to know at any given time. A lot of this information that we are and will be covering may be new to you and may require some adjustment in your thinking. But it is time to renew your mind with the truth.

The foundation and primary principle of your subconscious mind's work is based on your belief. Belief is transmitted from your *unconscious mind.* A belief, by definition, can be described as a thought that one continuously keeps thinking; also an idea or principle which one judges or accepts to be true.[7] We can call it the power of believing or the law of belief. Now, is the law of belief a scientific law or spiritual law? In a word . . . *yes*! It is actually both.

Let's consider the scientific law of belief first. As a scientific law, belief is a process that converts thoughts into reality. Belief is a most powerful component of a human being. Belief was, at one time, the subject matter for philosophers, but it now has become a prime subject for many psychologists and neuroscientists. Beliefs affect not only personal behaviors but also relationships as well.

Alok Jha reported in *The Guardian* on the topic of where belief is born. He writes,

> Scientists have begun to look in a different way at how the brain creates the convictions that mould our rela-

> tionships and inform our behavior. What was God's design for man to be able to develop belief? Under the physical scientific law, how does a belief exist in the brain? Beliefs and memories are similar but not equal . . . Memories are formed in the brain as networks of neurons are stimulated by an event. The more times the network is employed, the more it fires and the stronger the memory becomes.[8]

Peter Halligan, a psychologist at Cardiff University, states that belief takes the concept of memory a step further. He says that a belief is a mental architecture of how we interpret the world.[9]

In other words, our belief is an intellectual profile for how we perceive everything.

I submit to you that our beliefs originate from what we hear, see, and experience. And they intertwine with emotions, both consciously and subconsciously. Here is how it works according to a quote by Anton Chekhov: "Man is what he believes."[10]

In an article by the *Indian Journal of Psychiatry* entitled "The Biochemistry of Belief," it was documented that

> The sensory inputs we receive from the environment undergo a filtering process as they travel across one or more synapses, ultimately reaching the area of higher processing, like the frontal lobes. There the sensory information enters our conscious awareness. What portion of this sensory information that enters is determined by our beliefs. Fortunately for us, receptors on the cell membranes are flexible, which can alter in sensitivity and conformation. In other words, there is always a biochemical potential for change and possible growth. When we choose to change our thoughts (bursts of neurochemicals!), we become open and re-

> ceptive to other pieces of sensory information hitherto blocked by our beliefs! When we change our thinking, we change our beliefs. When we change our beliefs, we change our behavior.[11, 12]

We have just briefly covered some important aspects regarding the scientific law of belief. I believe God has given us the science behind "believing" to support the even more powerful spiritual law of belief, which we will cover next. So for the rest of this study, we will focus on the spiritual law of belief, which is clearly described in scripture. The power of believing is a key component to how the subconscious mind works. Your belief, or what you believe, is powerful . . . even miraculous! What Jesus spoke in Mark wraps it up and puts a bow on top, and it's worth repeating here:

> So Jesus answered and said to them, "Have faith in God. For assuredly, I say to you, whoever says to this mountain, 'Be removed and be cast into the sea,' and does not doubt in his heart, but believes that those things he says will be done, he will have whatever he says. Therefore I say to you, whatever things you ask when you pray, believe that you receive them, and you will have them."
> —Mark 11:22-24

The power is in believing! Jesus never spoke with any doubt. Every word He uttered was 100 percent belief and 0 percent doubt! He modeled the power of belief. We need to believe in the way God created our mind to work. Have faith in God, and believe in His purpose, intent, and design of your mind.

Faith in God and belief in Him as Deity (Creator and Supreme Being), both reside in the unconscious mind. Faith and belief in anything else also resides in the unconscious mind. Therefore, your unconscious mind is the primary guidance, navigation, and control system (PGNCS) for your words and actions. Just as the Apollo spacecraft was equipped with a self-contained guidance system that allowed the Apollo astronauts to carry out their missions when communications with Earth were interrupted, either as expected, when the spacecraft was behind the Moon, or in case of a communications failure. The PGNCS (and specifically its computer) were the command center for all system inputs. They were equipped and programmed for mission success! This is an example of your subconscious mind's function.[13]

You only have one mind, but God designed your mind with three very different and distinct functions. As previously stated, the conscious and the subconscious parts represent dual aspects of your mind. We will be making reference to these two aspects of the mind as we proceed through this study material. And we will finalize our study by addressing the unconscious part of the mind.

Now, I want you to consider your subconscious mind as a farm. When I was a young boy growing up on a farm, my fascination with the nature of seeds began to grow (pun intended). It is amazing to see how one seed can produce exponential increase. Seeds possess the essence of God.

> Anyone can count the seeds in an apple, but only God can count the apples in a seed. —Rev. Robert H. Schuller (1926–2015)

Therefore, I consider seeds to be divine. They demonstrate the nature of God. So again, consider your mind as a farm, and you are the farmer. Everybody knows that one of the farmer's main jobs is to sow seed. As the farmer of your subconscious farm (your mind), you are sowing seeds of thoughts in the field of your subconscious mind, all day, every day. What you sow as thought seeds in your subconscious mind, you will reap as a harvest in your physical body, your material universe, and your emotional well-being.

You can start right now to purposefully sow thoughts of wealth, health, happiness, success, love, peace, righteousness, and prosperity. Ponder these and other valuable attributes frequently, and graciously accept them with your objective and reasoning mind (conscious mind). It will greatly benefit you to diligently continue to sow these thought seeds in the field of your subconscious mind, and you will reap a bountiful harvest for your life.

The last four words of Philippians 4:8 read, "meditate on these things."

It is really important that you command and direct your thoughts and your thinking in a way that brings forth only the results that you desire:

> Do not let this Book of the Law depart from your mouth; meditate on it day and night, so that you may be careful to do everything written it. Then you will be prosperous and successful.
> —Joshua 1:8 NIV

This is a good place for me to share with you two illustrations that I believe will help you to relate to the workings of your mind. See below for the first illustration.

Count the Squares

How Many Squares Do You See?

There is no wrong answer because my question was, "How many squares do you see?" I did not ask you how many squares there are in the diagram. So, if the number of squares you see is less than the number of squares in the diagram, then you would be right, because that is the number of squares you see. However, if I were to tell you and show you the total number of squares in the diagram, you would be able to see an expanded version of what you originally and initially saw on your own.

There are actually thirty squares, and if you saw less than thirty squares, then get prepared for your mind to be expanded by new information, new thoughts, and a new way of thinking. Once you see the thirty squares, you will never see this diagram the same when you look at it again. If you live to be nine hundred years old, your subconscious mind will not let you see it the same! To see the thirty squares, view Appendix 1. Your subconscious mind awaits the truth.

Review the Answer Page for "Count the Squares" in Appendix 1.

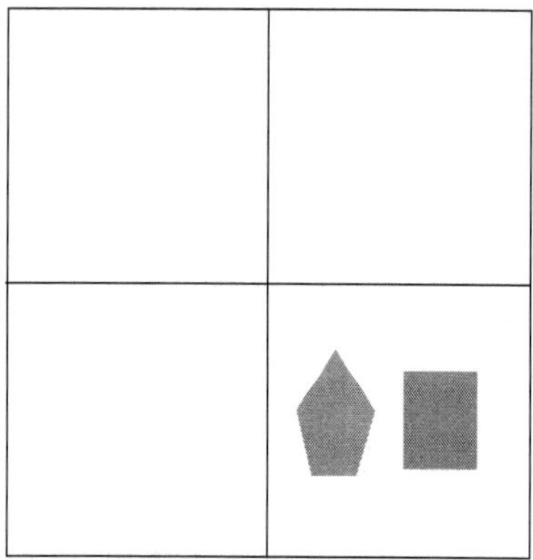

The pentagon image with five sides represents the farmhouse where I lived, and the rectangle image with four sides represents the garden that was adjacent to the house, which provided vegetables for family meals.

Using the diagram above, I want to explain how it represents the family farm that I lived on and how it also is a symbolic illustration of your mind.

The outer box in the diagram represents the acres of the farm (not to scale). The four quadrants represent the fields where different seeds are sown to produce different crops. The ground in each field of the farm does not care which seed you sow in it. Like your mind, it is going to produce the crop depending on the kind of seed you sowed. The ground in each field will not ask any questions, evaluate the age of the seeds, or make any determination about how much crop is to be produced. It will only take what you sow and produce an increase of the same kind. This is how your mind works with seeds of thoughts. What you think on the most will expand in your life. The seeds you sow in your subconscious mind will be the crop you grow in your life.

Words Are Seeds

Words are verbal expressions of thoughts, which again are seeds. When you program your subconscious mind with positive words and thoughts, and you come to an understanding of the truth about how the conscious and subconscious minds work, then your Divine Mind causes your thoughts to become agreeable with God's will. God instructs us in Philippians about the type of thoughts we should have.

> Finally, brethren, whatsoever things are true, whatsoever things are honest, whatsoever things are just, whatsoever things are pure, whatsoever things are lovely, whatsoever things are of good report; if there be any virtue, and if there be any praise, think on these things.
> —Philippians 4:8 KJV

When the words deposited into your subconscious mind line up with God's general description as laid out in Philippians 4:8, then your thoughts become agreeable with the will of

God. And the divine power of your subconscious mind will respond and bring to pass the best of all things thought and spoken by you. As you develop in the management and control of your thoughts and words, you will develop in the application of the power of your Divine Mind. You will get to the point that you are righteously partnering with the infinite power of the universe.

Understanding how your conscious and subconscious minds work together synergistically will empower you to receive the desires of your heart.

Remember, your subconscious mind is influenced by your conscious mind. Your subconscious mind acts on whatever your conscious mind presents. What you choose to focus on expands in your life—good or bad, positive or negative.

Again, whatever you focus on the *most* expands in your life. Thoughts can be spoon-fed to the subconscious mind through faith and repetition of words and images. So, if you can change your thoughts, you can change your life.

Everyone has a mind. There is a saying that a mind is a terrible thing to waste, but I say, a Divine Mind is a terrific thing to gain. Now since you already have a mind, you need to understand how it works, and you need to learn how to work it.

I want you to remember that the first two parts of your mind are the conscious and subconscious, and they work together. They are not two separate minds. They are simply two separate activities within one mind. Whatever you focus on with your thoughts, declare with your words, and believe in your heart, your subconscious mind will accept as true and bring it to pass. When your subconscious mind accepts your thoughts, words, and beliefs, your subconscious mind will cause it to come to pass.

You see, thoughts are things! And the thoughts that you entertain in your conscious mind will drop down into your subconscious mind, without any concentrated effort on your part. When that happens, your subconscious mind immediately proceeds to make it happen. It will tap into the Infinite Intelligence of the universe for its purpose. Your subconscious mind does not know the difference between what is true or false. It does not care, it does not judge; it just does what you suggest or tell it. Your subconscious mind is like a fertile garden that receives, accepts, and produces in the likeness of whatever seed you sow into it.[14]

All seeds are programmed to produce after their own kind. Your mind, just like a garden, has no choice . . . it must produce after its our kind. Be aware and conscious of the seeds you sow. Do not sow seeds for a crop you really do not want. If you have a rose garden, would you sow weed seeds?

Research has been done and tests have been run that validate the fact that your subconscious mind will accept any suggestion you give it, and if that suggestion is based on the Word of God, how much more powerful will the results be?!

Your life experiences up to this point have been based on the thoughts that have impacted and influenced your subconscious mind. Even if you have a history of imparting unwanted suggestions to your subconscious mind through wrong beliefs, the results can be reversed. However, it is a process.

It takes twenty-one days to form a new habit.[15] So the way to get rid of the weeds in the garden of your mind is to dig up or pull out the weeds. The weeds represent unwanted results from wrong thoughts and words. That is not God's best for you. You should develop confidence in your ability to reverse your results, based on God's Word:

> Therefore if any person is [ingrafted] in Christ (the Messiah) he is a new creation (a new creation altogether); the old [previous moral and spiritual condition] has passed away. Behold, the fresh and new has come!
> —2 Corinthians 5:17 AMPC

In Romans, we see God's way of reversing a situation. God's way is to call those things that are not as though they are! And because you are made in God's image, in His likeness, you can also call those things that are not as though they were!

> The God who gives life to the dead and calls things that are not as though they were.
> —Romans 4:17 NIV

If you don't like the way you are or a particular aspect of your life, you can make a conscious choice to change it. Remember, thoughts and words can create reality.

In Isaiah, God compares His ways and thoughts to our ways and thoughts. And God's ways involves words. And if you will pattern your ways, thoughts, and words after God's ways (speaking to situations), thoughts, and words, you will be operating in the likeness of God, getting God-like results. Do it by faith!

> "For my thoughts are not your thoughts, neither are your ways my ways," declares the Lord. "For as the heavens are higher than the earth, so are my ways higher than your ways and my thoughts than your thoughts. For as the rain and snow come down from

> heaven, and return not there again, but water the earth and make it bring forth and sprout, that it may give seed for the sower and bread for the eater, so shall my word be that goes forth from my mouth: it shall not return to me void [without producing any effect, useless], but it shall accomplish that which I please and purpose, and it shall prosper in the thing for which I sent it."
> —Isaiah 55:8-11

This passage of scripture in the book of Isaiah is a God Declaration! No one and nothing can spoil God's Word in any way that will cause it to be ineffective and fruitless. God's Word will not return to Him empty when declared out of the mouth of a believer. This scripture is not referring to man's word. It is referring to God's Word. The Bible tells us that God watches over His Word to perform it. So any other word does not carry the power to produce with God's guarantee. God wants us to declare His Word and apply it in our everyday life situations.

In the book of Job, God clearly announces the advantage and benefit of a declaration.

> You will also declare a thing, And it will be established for you; So light will shine on your ways.
> —Job 22:28 NKJV

God has provided us with a subconscious mind that is creative and connected to Him as our Divine source of Infinite Intelligence.

It is okay to personally declare that

> As the rain and snow come down from heaven, and do not return to it without watering the earth and making it bud and flourish, so that it yields seed for

> the sower and bread for the eater so is your spoken word that goes out from your mouth: It will not return unto you empty, but will accomplish what you desire and achieve the purpose for which you sent it.

It is good to speak that Word found in Isaiah 55:10–11 over your words!

CHAPTER 9:

Declarations and the Subconscious Mind

Watch your mouth! Don't carelessly declare anything you don't really want to have or happen. During World War II there was a slogan used by the United States Office of War Information. That slogan was "loose lips sink ships."[1] You may have heard that slogan at one time or another. There is a measure of truth in that declaration. My question to you is: what are you declaring?

Self-Divine Declaration

Self-divine declaration means declaring something definite and specific that is of, from, or by God, based on His Word, for yourself. Self-divine declaration is the act of declaring God's promise, will, and purpose for one's own life. It can be used to create a specific change in an area of your life that aligns with God's Word.

Your subconscious is totally receptive and obedient to verbal instructions, statements, and suggestions you give it; it can also change behavior, conditions, and emotions. You can even reverse the results of negative suggestions that you have induced into your subconscious by involuntary neglect, careless spoken words, or damaging default.

Practice Practical Application

The practice of repeating divine declarations daily will keep you on your way. On your way to where? On your way to accomplishing your desire and achieving your purpose. Repeat your divine declaration statements each day at the most receptive times for your subconscious mind. The two most receptive times when the subconscious is most available are at night just before you fall asleep and first thing in the morning when you first awake. Do these two times every day as a minimum. Practice doing this every day for at least twenty-one days. You may also consider some form of fasting during this initial period. Putting this practice into play will counteract the conditions manifested from negative verbal statements made in the past. Negative words that produce undesired results in your life.

God has given you power to negate the negative suggestions that your subconscious mind has received and acted upon. You have to choose to overpower the negative seeds that have been sown through wrong thoughts, words, pictures, videos, electronic games, news stories, life experiences, negative statements of others, music, etc.

Here's an encouraging statement I'd like to share with you: "Don't let anyone else's negative opinion become your reality." The statements of others, in and of themselves, positive or negative, actually have no power to affect your life outside of the power you give them through your own thoughts of acceptance. If you allow the thoughts and words of others to impregnate your subconscious mind, you will sabotage your own good. The way to experience your good and have your desires is to practice repetitive divine declarations. Remember, your predominant thoughts, whatever you think about continuously and focus on the most, expand in your life and become your reality.

In chapter 20, we will cover how to develop and document declarations that are right for you personally.

Subconscious Miracle Working Power

There is divine power working with your subconscious mind! And it works endlessly and without ceasing . . . *ever*! It never sleeps, even though you do. It keeps working while you sleep. It never needs to take time to eat, take a bathroom break, or rest. It never gets tired or goes on vacation. It can guide you and it can provide solutions to any problem. Your subconscious mind is always on the job! It is never inactive. In fact, it controls the functions of all vital systems in your body which keep you alive.

The source of the Infinite Intelligence working with your subconscious mind is the same source of power that hung the moon and lit the stars. It is the same source that keeps all planets in the universe on course and keeps the waters of the oceans in their place. The Infinite Intelligence working through your subconscious mind is the source of divine—inspired ideas, creative concepts and superior strategies. It is the source of wealth and riches, happiness, and success. It is the source of hunches, notions, and unctions that guide, instruct, and direct you, as the following well-known statement expresses: "Something told me to (or not to) ________" *(fill in the blank with a personal experience).*

The Word of God addresses where the Holy Spirit, the anointing, the unction, resides and abides:

> But ye have <u>an unction</u> from the Holy One, and ye know all things.
> —1 John 2:20 KJV

My footnote to this verse is: To *know all things* is having Infinite Intelligence.

> But <u>the anointing</u> which ye have received of Him <u>abideth in you</u>...
> —1 John 2:27

The New King James Version reads as follows:

> But you have an anointing from the Holy One, and you know all things.... But the anointing which you have received from Him abides in you...
> —1 John 2:20, 27

The Amplified Bible increases the clarity and expands the understanding of these two verses of scripture in a way that I want to point out here. The Amplified Bible basically explains that you have been appointed by the Holy One, which means you hold a sacred appointment from the Holy One, and you have been given an unction from the Holy One. It also explains in verse 27 that the anointing (the sacred appointment and the unction) that you have received from Him abides permanently in you.

Now to answer the question of where in you does the Holy Spirit live? We have already studied and discovered, that both the Hebrew and Greek words for "heart" and "mind" are the same. With that being said, we see that The Living Bible summarizes it this way:

> But you have received the Holy Spirit and He lives within you, in your hearts . . .
> —1 John 2:27

CHAPTER 10:

Think Right for Your Money Type

Your financial success is not determined by hard work or long hours. Consider the following:

> And you shall remember the LORD your God, for it is He who gives you power to get wealth.
> —Deuteronomy 8:18 NKJV

There is a quote that is relevant here. It was made by William James (1842–1910), who was an American philosopher and psychologist who was also trained as a physician. The first educator to offer a psychology course in the United States, James was labeled the "Father of American Psychology." He said:

> The power to move the world is in the subconscious mind.[1]

It was stated earlier that your subconscious mind is one with God and Holy Spirit. In general, people do not understand the interrelationship and interaction between their

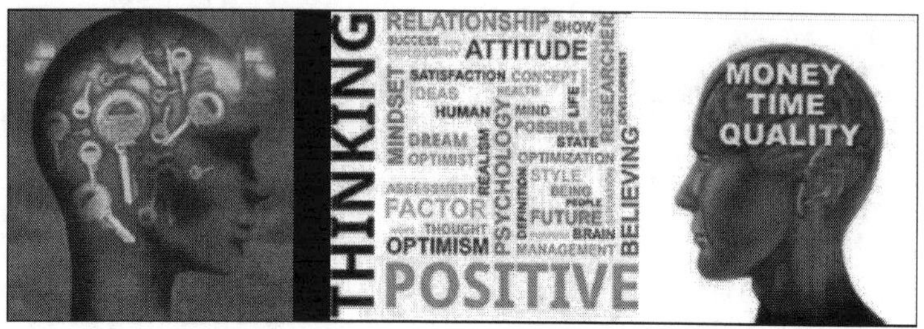

conscious and subconscious minds. The interesting thing is that your subconscious mind does not care if you know how it works or not . . . it just responds automatically to bring about results. Let me give you a couple of examples where, knowingly or unknowingly, impressions are made on the subconscious mind.

First, I want you to consider where your perception of money actually begins.

The Formation of Money Habits

Are your money memories, habits, behaviors, attitudes, and beliefs impacting your financial success, or the lack thereof?

Whether you are at a point in your life where you believe this or not, it has proven true for many people. What you think affects your reality. Your experiences, your influences, and your beliefs from childhood can and do influence your choices and decisions as an adult.

Money Habits Are Formed and Set by Age Seven

A Cambridge University research study suggests that most young children had grasped all the main aspects of how money works and formed "core behaviors which they will take into adulthood, and which will affect financial decisions they make during the rest of their lives." Therefore, the Cambridge University report highlights the power of parents to foster money skills and core behaviors at home. Parents must not underestimate the effect of their own good (and bad) money habits and the impact they will have on their children.[2]

Whether we realize it or not, how we were raised has a tremendous impact on how we make decisions as adults. Sometimes the results are positive, certainly. But other times, the results are detrimental to our well-being, especially when it comes to our financial health. This doesn't mean that we can just blame Mom or Dad (or both) for our money mistakes and leave it at that. But once we understand the root of our bad habits and poor decisions, we can take ownership of them and make a conscious and intentional effort to change them.

As children, we begin to form our beliefs and attitudes about money through value-laden messages that are passed on to us by our parents, grandparents, and society. As a personal financial analyst and master certified financial coach, I refer to these as "money memories."

What Can Money Memories Teach Us?

Our money memories help us to gain insight into the things that have consciously and subconsciously influenced how we think and feel about money—and how we handle finances.

In order to move forward and navigate life with greater financial confidence as adults, we must look back. After all, a belief is nothing more than a thoroughly practiced thought in which trust and confidence is placed in some person or thing.

And that can take place on the conscious and subconscious levels.[3]

Second, I want you to consider the power of your imagination.

CHAPTER 11:

The Power of Imagination

Your imagination can make a huge difference, as witnessed in this stunning true story of Captain Jerry Coffee, a prisoner of war (POW) for seven years and nine days in Hanoi . . . in the Communist prisons of North Vietnam.

While flying reconnaissance missions over North Vietnam, piloting his jet fighter, Capitan Coffee was shot down by enemy fire. After parachuting to safety, he was captured by enemy forces on the ground.

During all the many horrific years as a POW, Captain Coffee maintained his sanity by playing a mental game of golf every day. Other than his amazing survival as a prisoner of war, the most interesting aspect of his story is that by playing an imaginary round of golf in his mind each day during his captivity, he found upon his release that he had markedly improved his game.[1]

You can use your imagination to improve your financial posture. Imagine how your financial life would be if you had no debt.

Your imagination has the power to elevate and serve not only your financial success but also success in every area of your life where it is applied.

Mind Your Money Business

Thinking about money the way God thinks about money is the first step to financial success. The way you think about money will forge your relationship with money. And your relationship with money will drive the decisions you make regarding money. Consequently, your money thoughts will determine your level of financial success.

Let's consider seven keys to financial success, based on the Word of God.

1. Do not love money.

> For the love of money is a root of all kinds of evil, for which some have strayed from the faith in their greediness, and pierced themselves through with many sorrows.
> —1 Timothy 6:10

Money is not the root of all kinds of evil, but it is the love of money. It is better to love what you can accomplish with money, rather than the money itself. Money can be very temporary, but what you do with the money can be eternal.

2. Do not become a slave to debt.

> The rich rules over the poor, and the borrower is the slave of the lender.
> —Proverbs 22:7 ASV

Debt is the biggest threat to your financial success. If you have debt, establish a plan to eliminate it as soon as possible.

3. Do not cosign on any debt obligation.

> Unless you have the extra cash on hand, don't countersign a note. Why risk everything you own? They'll even take your bed!
> —Proverbs 22:26-27 TLB

> It is poor judgment to countersign another's note, to become responsible for his debts.
> —Proverbs 17:18

Cosigning on a debt for someone else is not a recommended financial decision.

4. Do not rob God.

> "Will a man rob God? Yet you have robbed Me! But you say, 'In what way have we robbed You?' In tithes and offerings. You are cursed with a curse, For you have robbed Me, Even this whole nation. Bring all the tithes into the storehouse, That there may be food in My house, And try Me now in this," Says the LORD of hosts, "If I will not open for you the windows of heaven And pour out for you such blessing That there will not be room enough to receive it. And I will rebuke the devourer for your sakes, So the he will not destroy the fruit of your ground, Nor shall the vine fail to bear fruit for you in the field," Says the Lord of hosts; "And all nations will call you blessed, For you will be a delightful land," Says the LORD of hosts.
> —Malachi 3:8-12 NKJV

Never forget or deny that the tithe belongs to God and it is holy. So if you honor God with your obedience to the first 10 percent, which is holy, then it causes the other 90 percent to be holy. You can also expect overflowing blessings from a faithful God.

5. Create increase by giving.

> Give, and it will be given to you. They will pour into your lap a good measure—pressed down, shaken together, and running over [with no space left for more]. For with the standard of measurement you use [when you do good to others], it will be measured to you in return.
> —Luke 6:38 AMP

Remember the words of the Lord Jesus, how He said, "It is more blessed to give than to receive" (Acts 20:35 KJV).

6. Knowledge and understanding leads to riches.

> Through skillful and godly wisdom a house [a life, a home, a family] is built, And by understanding it is established [on a sound and good foundation], And by knowledge its rooms are filled With all precious and pleasant riches.
> —Proverbs 24:3-4 AMP

> Listen carefully and hear the words of the wise, And apply your mind to my knowledge; For it will be pleasant if you keep them in mind [incorporating them as guiding principles]; Let them be ready on your lips [to guide and strengthen yourself and others].
> —Proverbs 22:17-18

It is necessary to gain knowledge about how money works in order to better manage it and have success with it. This knowledge will not come by chance, it comes by choice. You must choose to learn and apply the knowledge you gain. There is a popular saying that "knowledge is power." But that is not true. Knowledge is potential, and applied knowledge is power. Position and prepare yourself to have financial success, and train your children to do the same.

7. Find safety and victory in counsel.

> Where there is no [wise, intelligent] guidance, the people fall [and go off course like a ship without a helm], But in the abundance of [wise and godly] counselors there is victory.
> —Proverbs 11:14

Typically, schools (public, private, charter, and Christian) have not offered courses on money management or understanding how money works. Therefore, it is up to each individual to get educated in this very necessary area. Your chances of success with money hinges on your level of knowledge and understanding.

The relationship that you develop with money by your thoughts, your words, and your actions will determine the level of your financial success. There is a financial synergistic concept that I share in my coaching practice, which we refer to as the "Mx^3 Factor." I just want to briefly explain an introduction to this extremely powerful concept.

The definition of "synergistic" is "relating to the interaction or cooperation of two or more organizations, substances, or other agents to produce a combined effect greater than the sum of their separate effects."[2] The synergistic interaction of the Mx^3 Factor involves three "M" components. They are <u>mind</u>, <u>mouth</u>, and <u>money</u>. In mathematics, x^3 is called an exponential expression where x is a constant (called the base) and "3" is the exponent and indicates the expressed <u>power</u> of the base. I do not want to go any deeper into the math. I just want to simplify the message here. The x is a constant. Who is the most constant person in the universe? Almight God!

When you employ your mind and engage your mouth (which contains the power of your tongue), and you direct and release that power on your target (your money), a synergy takes place that has exponentially greater results.

So it is beneficial to think and speak about money in a way that serves your financial success. It would also be wise to get help from a certified financial coach to help develop a plan and practical applications for taking control and managing your money.

CHAPTER 12:

How to Apply Divine Mind Power

Remember what we said earlier . . . your subconscious mind is always active and working, day and night. It never rests nor sleeps. You should keep your conscious mind engaged in the activity of impressing upon your subconscious mind expectations of the best, and make sure that the thoughts you habitually think are based on whatsoever things are lovely, true, just, and of good report. Today you can begin to direct your conscious mind, knowing that your subconscious mind is always communicating, creating, and reproducing according to your habitual thinking. You can use the power of your subconscious for wealth, health, happiness, success, love, peace, harmony, healing, prosperity, etc.

There is a creative force that only goes to work when there is an established thought that is supported by imagination, visualization, trust, and belief in the power of the subconscious mind to fulfill your need or desire. Since the spirit of God resides in the heart and mind of a believer, their desire becomes God's desire. In Psalm 37:4 and Psalm 20:4, the Word of God says that He will give you the desires of your heart and make all your plans succeed.

Every born-again believer who understands and applies the knowledge of a Divine Mind will get the results hoped for by faith. By Infinite Intelligence within your Divine Mind, you can achieve and receive your directed desires. The power of God is available to operate through your Divine Mind. Believe it and act like it!

Scientists understand that the subconscious has a vital role in what they consider the power or magic of believing. But born-again believers understand that the Divine Mind is the only ultimate source of power for what we believe. Deuteronomy 8:18 tells us to remember the Lord our God, for it is He who gives us power to get wealth. You remember with your conscious mind, and God gives you power through your subconscious mind. Also, faith is connected to the subconscious mind, so you must be diligent to believe in the wisdom, ability, and power of the subconscious to do what God designed it to do.

> Keep this Book of the Law always on your lips; meditate on it day and night, so that you may be careful to do everything written in it. Then you will be prosperous and successful.
> —Joshua 1:8 NIV

I like the way the Amplified Bible reads in Joshua. God wants us to be confident in our doing what He has commanded us to do, and then He tells us why we should be confident.

> This Book of the Law shall not depart out of your mouth, but you shall meditate on it day and night, that you may observe and do according to all that is written in it. For then you shall make your way prosperous, and then you shall deal wisely and have good success. Have not I commanded you? Be strong, vigorous, and very courageous. Be not afraid, neither be dismayed, for the Lord your God is with you wherever you go.
> —Joshua 1:8-9 AMPC

Here are a few key points to consider in these two verses, in the light of what we have studied thus far.

1. God did not make a suggestion in these verses. He commanded and we need to obey. He has given us the key to our success.
2. We are to think, give thought to, and speak according to God's Word.
3. We are to observe and do according to what we think and speak. Because what we think and say will have a profound impact on what we see and how we act.
4. I believe that what God commanded us is in verse 8, not verse 9. Verse 9 contains God's encouragement and confidence building. Verse 8 has all the "shall(s)," whereas verse 9 has the confidence builders, with the ultimate confidence builder being His promise to be with us wherever we go. How? In our minds! Everywhere we go, our mind goes. You will never leave home without it . . . it is forever and always with you. Because God resides in your mind, He is always with you at all times.

Your divine subconscious mind will not operate from thoughts and words of unbelief. There is no positive or beneficial power in unbelief. When programming your need or desire in your subconscious, you need to understand and believe that it is a spiritual work that has already been done. So see yourself with your need met or desire fulfilled. See yourself already successful. Jesus said in Mark 9:23 (NKJV), "If you can believe, all things are possible to him who believes."

Remember, whatever you focus your thoughts and imagination on, or whatever you primarily think about continuously, like thoughts in a loop, is what expands in your life and becomes your reality. So be sure to tighten your mental grip and hold on to a mental image or a vision of what you want. This is so very important to do. How important, you ask? Read below:

> Where there is no vision, the people perish: but he that keepeth the law, happy is he.
> —Proverbs 29:18 KJV

We need to establish a redemptive revelation of God and His Divine Mind design to gain knowledge and understanding of how it works. Why? Because God said He will reject us and ignore our children, if we reject knowledge.

> <u>My people are destroyed for lack of knowledge</u>. Because you have ejected knowledge, I also will reject you from being priest for Me; Because you have forgotten the law of your God, I also will forget your children.
> —Hosea 4:6 NKJV

What you have been learning about "Divine Mind Works" is right from the Word of God, which is part of God's Law.

The Power of Repetition

The definition of "repetition" is the action of repeating something that has already been said, written, or done; it is the recurrence of an action or event.[1]

Repetition is also an important element of practice, and the mechanics of repetition is key to the fundamental rhythm of improvement and ultimate success. There is a phrase that says, "Practice makes perfect." The simplicity of this phrase implies that the more you practice, the better your skills become. I do not agree that practice makes perfect. You can practice wrongly, and it will make you perfectly wrong. No matter how much one practices anything, 100 percent perfection for all time is statistically improbable. However, I do believe that practice makes permanent, right or wrong.

When it comes to the subconscious mind, it is the repeated declarations that get God's attention and create a paradigm shift in thought patterns that generate transformational change. It is the continuous repeating of the same conscious thought that causes that thought to be planted or programmed into your subconscious mind and the subconscious minds of others. A repeated suggestion has the power to create the reality of a need or desire.

> Let them shout for joy, and be glad, that favour my righteous cause: yea, let them say continually, Let the LORD be magnified, which hath pleasure in the prosperity of His servant.
> —Psalm 35:27 KJV

Try saying this often: "Lord, I magnify You and take delight in the pleasure You have in my prosperity." This is a powerful declaration! Remember, Psalm 37:4 tells us to delight ourselves in the Lord, and He will give us the desires of our heart.

Other repetitive activity will also get results.

> And so I tell you, keep on asking, and you will receive what you ask for. Keep on seeking, and you will find. Keep on knocking, and the door will be opened to you.
> —Luke 11:9 NLT

CHAPTER 13:

Creativity and Your Subconscious Mind

The source of creativity is God Almighty, but the seat of creativity is your subconscious mind! The subconscious mind is the engine that powers creative imagination.

The power of creative imagination goes virtually untapped and unused by most of the people in the world. The capacity and power of creative imagination is deliberately and purposefully applied by just a small percentage of people. Those who do discover its application become the recipients of divine-inspired ideas, plans, creative concepts, superior strategies, and witty inventions. All insights, revelations, inspirations, dreams, and visions come through the creative imagination center of the subconscious mind. The imagination is the production center of the mind.

The subconscious mind registers and records everything experienced, encountered, or exposed through the five senses. This means that it retains what you see, hear, taste, smell, and touch. You can choose to voluntarily program your subconscious mind with any plan, purpose, goal, or thought that you desire to convert into a physical, material, or emotional equivalent. Your subconscious mind is triggered by the predominate thoughts that are mixed with vision, words, belief, and imagination.

The Bible tells us in Hebrews 11:1 that faith is the substance of things hoped for, the evidence of things not seen . . . with the natural eye, that is. I submit to you that hope is a product of your mind. Faith activates the subconscious mind and makes a connection with Infinite Intelligence that we know as "God" and Holy Spirit.

The subconscious mind never rests, slumbers, or sleeps. And in ways that are unexplainable by man and science, the subconscious mind taps into the power of the Infinite Intelligence of God Almighty, our Creator. The subconscious mind will automatically transform thoughts and desires into reality.

Your subconscious mind is always available and forever connected to you. You can choose to purposefully program any desire that you wish to be transformed into reality. Psalm 37:4 says that if we take delight or delight yourself in the Lord, He will give you the desires of your heart.

The subconscious mind is the link between God's Divine Infinite Intelligence and the conscious mind of man. It is the link through which we can access the power and vastness of God's Divine Infinite Intelligence. This is where conscious thoughts are transformed into spiritual realities. The subconscious mind is the link that empowers righteous prayer to be received and answered by the sole source and provider of answered prayer.

> Don't copy the behavior and customs of his world, but let God transform you into a new person by changing the way you think. Then you will learn to know God's will for you, which is good and pleasing and perfect.
> —Romans 12:2

Therefore, do not conform, but be transformed, and learn to obey God's Word and to do God's will.

Creative Production

How do you activate and employ your subconscious mind for creative production? First, consider the unlimited capacity and potential of the subconscious mind for creative productivity. When it comes to the power to be creative, your biggest and most valuable asset is your Divine Mind.

When you get to the point where you embrace the reality and the power of a Divine Mind to transform thoughts into reality, you will understand the possibilities and importance of managing its input with righteous desires.

> Take delight in the Lord, and He will give you the desires of your heart.
> —Psalm 37:4 NIV

> You have granted him his heart's desire and have not withheld the request of his lips.
> —Psalm 21:2

> He fulfills the desires of those who fear him, He hears their cry and saves them.
> —Psalm 145:19

> But seek first his kingdom and his righteousness, and all these things will be given to you as well.
> —Matthew 6:33

Remember, the subconscious mind operates on its own and needs no assistance from you to motivate and influence it. It is designed to function on autopilot. With that being said, please understand that the mere fact that you are reading, hearing, or watching this material, or subjecting your subconscious mind to any other positive content, is an activity of programming.

Thoughts are seed, and seeds are preprogrammed to produce specifically after their own kind. Thoughts stimulate and activate the subconscious mind. So thoughts of fear will produce fear as a reality in your life. Thoughts of victory and success will produce victory and success as a reality in your life. These thought seeds are preprogrammed to produce the same thing. The best action you can take is to program your subconscious with desirable thoughts.

God did not create the subconscious mind to be inactive at any time. He created it to operate continuously, without ceasing. The subconscious mind is always hungry and is feeding at all times. If you fail to feed it desirous thoughts, then it will feed on any other thoughts that it receives from other sources, due to your neglect and omission. Your mind is perpetually receiving both positive and negative thoughts and images from various sources, without your awareness, but not without your permission. By your omission, you give permission. Some are good sources and some are bad sources. Some are desirable and some are undesirable.

With the knowledge you are gaining about how a Divine Mind works, God is now holding you responsible for better management and control of thought seeding to your subconscious mind. The influence of negative seeds should be minimized, and the influence of positive seeds should be maximized.

Nothing has ever been created without the influence of a thought. All creative production begins with a thought. Progresses through words and proceeds with action.

A Word About Your Words

Remember that words spoken have creative power! But words without faith or corresponding action simply diminish the power of the words spoken. There are several physical components that contribute to the production of a spoken word. It is difficult for words to be spoken clearly without some of these. Here is a short list: mouth, tongue, lips, teeth, vocal cords. All of these help to produce the sound of a spoken word. There are also a few nonphysical components that contribute to a spoken word, no matter what language. Here are a few: air/breath, pitch, tone, frequency, volume, vibration. As you can see, the production of spoken words requires a network of components that work together synergistically.[1]

As you might imagine, the power of spoken words can be maximized with the addition of faith and belief. The Bible is full of examples and stories that support this truth. What kind of power are we talking about? Well, according to scripture, it's the power of life and death, good and evil, blessing and cursing, abundance and lack, positive and negative, and having and having not. Your words will deliver results in the likeness of what you spoke.

> Death and life are in the power of the tongue, And those who love it will eat its fruit.
> —Proverbs 18:21 NKJV

> Death and life are in the power of the tongue, and they who indulge it shall eat the fruit of it [for death or life].
> —Proverbs 18:21 AMPC

The tongue has been used as an instrument to bless and curse for as long as people have communicated and interacted with each other. The choice and power to bless or curse is yours and mine. So choose blessing, and choose life.

> Out of the same mouth come both blessing and cursing. These things, my brothers, should not be this way [for we have a moral obligation to speak in a manner that reflects our fear of God and profound respect for His precepts].
> —James 3:10 AMPC

Words have contained creative power since the beginning of time. God used words when He created the heavens and the earth. This is supported by scripture in the first chapter of Genesis:

> In the beginning God created the heavens and the earth.
> —Genesis 1:1 NKJV

We also read,

> By faith we understand that the worlds were framed by the word of God, so that the things which are seen were not made of things which are visible.
> —Hebrews 11:3

God spoke the worlds into existence, as evidenced in scripture, in the first chapter of the book of Genesis (NIV): "And God said, 'Let there be light,' and there was light." The literal Hebrew says, "God said, 'Light will be,' and light was."[2]

The words "and God said" appear ten times in the first chapter of Genesis.[3] To the natural mind, these words become repetitive and somewhat monotonous. But, through spiritual understanding, we will realize that God wanted it written that way to bring attention to just how absolutely essential words were to the process of creation. The same understanding of repetition applies to the programming of the subconscious mind.

Each time God spoke the words "Let there be," whatever followed those words became a reality. Each time God spoke, He released His faith with creative power to manifest what He spoke. God created all things by the power of His Word, and, according to Hebrews 1:3, He is still upholding all things by the word of His power. God's words always produce what He says.

> For as the rain comes down, and the snow from heaven, And do not return there, But water the earth, And make it bring forth and bud, That it may give seed to the sower And bread to the eater, So shall My word be that goes forth from My mouth; It shall not return to Me void, But it shall accomplish what I please, And it shall prosper in the thing for which I send it.
> —Isaiah 55:10–11

God created the earth and everything on it and in it; then He said, "Let us make man in Our image, after our likeness: and let them have dominion over the fish of the sea, and over the fowl of the air, and over the cattle, and over all the earth, and over every creeping thing that creeps upon the earth" (Gen 1:26 KJV). So God created man in his own image, in the image of God created "He him; male and female created He them" (Gen. 1:27).

The very instant that God spoke these words in verse 26 of Genesis chapter 1 is the instant that man became alive. Man was created from the faith-filled words of God . . . words of power, dominion, and life. These words came out of the inward most nature of God and His thoughts, where the original dominion, authority, and power exist. All of the power required for man to have dominion and authority over the earth was already a part of man from the very beginning. Man was created out of that original power.

Adam was created in the same class as God. By that, I mean he was made in the image and likeness of God. When God said, "Be fruitful, multiply, replenish, subdue, and have dominion" (see Genesis 1:28), He made a covenant with man. Man was created with power; then God gave him authority to use that power by making a covenant with him, guaranteeing him dominion over this earth.

Man was to rule by speaking words. His words would carry the power and anointing of God that was in him from the time he was first created. God places a high priority on words. He has never done anything without saying it first, as witnessed in chapter 1 of Genesis. God's faith-filled word was the original force in the universe.

Before Jesus came to the earth, God spoke His Word and then spoke His Word again and again and again. This method of repetitive speaking was established by God, and it will work for us as well when we apply it to our affirmations and declarations in programming our subconscious minds. How many times did God say the Messiah was coming? It was prophesied for over a thousand years. God kept saying He is coming. The circumstances on Earth made it look as if there was no way He could accomplish it; but He just kept on saying it. He would not be moved by what He saw.

Remember, we are made in His likeness. Once that word was received by a man, it was here to stay. God would not relent, and neither should we! Repetition gives power to spoken words in declarations and affirmations. Repeated suggestions that program the subconscious mind will manifest results, just like it did for God.

Your tongue is the controlling element in your life. No matter how bad the storm or how severe the problem is, your tongue can change the situation. No situation, condition, or circumstance is so big that you, as a born-again believer, cannot overcome it with the Word of God in your mouth.

I want you to consider the words of Jesus in Matthew 6:31 where He says, "Therefore take no thought, saying, What shall we eat? or, What shall we drink? or, Wherewithal shall we be clothed?"

In this verse, Jesus connects the power of words with the seeds of thought. You first take the thought and then you <u>say</u> it. Whether thoughts are positive and righteous or negative and evil, they are planted and take root in the mind. As they are meditated on persistently, they will drop down from the conscious into the subconscious and finally come out of the mouth at some time.

The subconscious is like the heart, and the Word of God says that out of the abundance of the heart, the mouth will speak. Thoughts that are spoken into your spirit repeatedly will be in there in abundance, and the same words will come out of your spirit through your mouth without your mind having to call for them. They will be on autopilot. Those are the words that are filled with the power of either faith or fear, love or hate, or success or failure. Whatever thoughts you have been verbalizing will take root and produce fruit according to the words you have spoken.

It is worth the investment of time and effort to sow positive thoughts on purpose, rather than allowing negative thoughts to take control by default or omission. The power of your tongue and the words of your mouth—whether good or evil, life or death, or blessing or cursing—will manifest itself in your life. Read the following words of Jesus:

> After Jesus called the crowd to Him, He said, "Listen and understand this: It is not what goes into the mouth of a man that defiles and dishonors him, but what comes out of the mouth, this defiles and dishonors him." . . . But whatever [word] comes out of the mouth comes from the heart, and this is what defiles and dishonors the man."
> —Matthew 15:10-11, 18 AMP

There are many people who have been raised and influenced since very early childhood to speak words of lack, sickness, failure, death, and other negative expressions. In your everyday communications, you may be unconsciously using negative words that give life and power to fear, doubt, and unbelief. Words like, "It scared me to death, I was tickled to death, I laughed so hard I thought I would die, I am dying to see them, I am so sick and tired of this, I believe I am going to be sick, I cannot afford that, I seriously doubt that" . . . and the list goes on and on.

I find this type of behavior prolific, especially in the area of finances, where people continue to question why God is not providing their needs or blessing them. They nullify God's desire to bless them by the words that come out of their own mouths. They actively obstruct God's provision by the power of their tongue. Without realizing it, you could be making negative statements that give energy and life and set into motion opposing forces that diminish your quality of life and block your provision.

Practice speaking God's Word and His promises as declarations of faith. Personalize God's Word for every area of your life.

The spiritual principle of Mark 11:22 is basic to your life as a born-again believer. This is how God uses His faith. Jesus Himself said, "Have faith in God," or as the cross-reference says, "Have the faith *of* God." Then He continued to explain how the faith of God works. <u>The faith of God works by "saying."</u>

Notice the close connection between confessing with the mouth and believing with the heart. Jesus explains this in the book of Mark:

> Whosoever shall say unto this mountain, Be thou removed, and be thou cast into the sea; and shall not doubt in his heart, but shall believe that those things which he saith shall come to pass; he shall have whatsoever he saith.
> —Mark 11:23 KJV

Jesus is not talking about Himself here. He is talking about you and me: we are the "whosoever."

Jesus said you are either justified or condemned by the words that come out of your mouth. There is a high value placed on words, and they are powerful. There is an old expression that says, "Sticks and stones may break my bones, but words will never hurt me." That expression is *so* not true. Words can hurt you more than any sticks and stones. The pain may be different, but the pain is real and can last a lifetime.

Remember, your words are birthed and emerge from your thoughts. Before anything is spoken, it begins as a thought. Philippians addresses *how* to think:

> Finally, brethren, whatsoever things are true, whatsoever things are honest, whatsoever things are just, whatsoever things are pure, whatsoever things are lovely, whatsoever things are of good report; if there be any virtue, and if there be any praise, think on these things.
> —Philippians 4:8

Voiceprint in the Atmosphere

All things in our universe are constantly in motion, vibrating. Even objects that appear to be stationary are in fact vibrating, oscillating, and resonating at various frequencies.

Here is an interesting scientific side note: Every piece of matter has a resonance frequency or series of frequencies because all matter is made up of atoms. Atoms are formed by electromagnetic waves that have a specific frequency. When these atoms form a larger piece of matter, the frequency of the electromagnetic waves is the frequency of that matter.[4] This is both interesting and educational.

After God said "Let us make man in our image, after our likeness," He created Adam. The atoms used to create Adam were God's atoms with His specific frequency. So here we can see the power and significance of the combined science and spirit behind frequency. Frequency exists in stuff you can see, as well as stuff you cannot see. It is true that the most important things in life are invisible. It generally requires the use of special electronic equipment to display frequency in a way that it can be seen and measured.

God created sound along with everything else in the universe. It was the sound of His voice that created the heavens and the earth. Sound is a type of energy made by vibrations. Sound energy is produced when an object vibrates. The sound vibrations cause waves of pressure that travel through a medium, such as air, water, wood, or metal. Sound energy is a form of mechanical energy.[5]

The vocal cords produce sound when they come together and then vibrate as air passes through them during exhalation of air from the lungs. This vibration produces the sound wave for your voice. This is your individual voiceprint.[6]

Frequency is a key element in all matter. It is also a key element in communications. Frequency is the secret to establishing and maintaining a communication connection with God. If we are not on the same frequency with God, then it is very difficult to communicate. How can two communicate unless they transmit and receive on the same frequency? Have you ever tried to listen to a radio station and you can't quit get on the right frequency? The station has a lot of static or noise and is hard to understand. Then, when you finally get on the right frequency, everything comes through loud and clear. It is very refreshing.

A voiceprint is an individually distinctive pattern of certain voice characteristics that is spectrographically produced.[7] It is a visual record of speech, analyzed with respect to frequency, duration, and amplitude.

Your voiceprint is like your personal vocal signature or the vocal equivalent of your fingerprint. In fact, your voiceprint is as individually unique as your fingerprint.[8] And, of all the billions or trillions of voices in the universe, God knows your individually unique voice, and He is always listening for your voiceprint. God always hears your voice and knows that it is you speaking. So you need to be mindful of what you say and how you say it. What you say comes from your mind, but how you say it comes from your heart.

There is so much more about the importance and power of our spoken words that could be included here, but it would take another full book to cover it all. I strongly encourage you to manage your choice of words and establish your God given voiceprint. Also listen for His voice. Stay tuned to His frequency.

CHAPTER 14:

Where Is Your Faith?

Where is your faith? This is important to understand. It is the same question that Jesus asked His disciples in Luke where He calmed the storm. Even the wind and waves obeyed the words spoken by Jesus in faith.

> "Where is your faith?" he asked his disciples. In fear and amazement they asked one another, "Who is this? He commands even the winds and the water, and they obey him."
> —Luke 8:25 NIV

Where is *your* faith? There are two ways to consider this question. The first is to consider on what or *in* what you place your faith. This would typically be a thing or a person. The second consideration of this question "Where is your faith?" relates to the place or space that faith occupies or resides. This second consideration is what I want to address with you very briefly. It is critical that we understand the place or space of faith and belief. Where is your faith? Where do you believe? Or rather, "from where does your faith and belief come?"

In Matthew 14:31 (Jesus Walks on the Water), consider what Jesus said to Peter: "You of little faith, why did you doubt?" This verse gives a clue as to where faith is. You see, fear, doubt, and unbelief are all different states of mind. They occupy space in your mind.

The second question Jesus asked in Matthew 14:31 is "Why did you doubt?" This question actually aligns with the question we considered in Luke 8:25 where fear is confronted. Matthew 14:31 addresses "doubt."

Fear and doubt occupy space in one's mind. Remember that fear is a state of mind, and so is doubt. So, if fear, doubt, and unbelief are negative states of mind, then faith and belief have got to be a positive state of mind. Therefore, the answer to the question of "Where is your faith?" is clear: it's in your mind. Faith occupies space and is resident in your mind. Specifically, your subconscious mind.

Now faith is the substance of things hoped for. Hope is also a state of mind. Both of these truths again confirm that faith occupies space in the mind. State of mind is defined as the psychological state of someone's cognitive processes at a certain time; the condition or character of a person's thoughts or feelings.[1]

Why is it so important to understand where your faith is? I think it clarifies how God intended for us to operate, in faith and believing. It's important to understand the relationship between the mind, the heart, and the spirit, as we have laid out and covered in this material. Hebrews 11:6 explains that without faith it is impossible to please God, for whoever comes to

Him must believe that He exists and that He rewards those who diligently seek Him.

Eternity Mindset

Are you programmed for departure? There is one guarantee about this life on earth, and that is, you will not get out of it alive (at least, in the natural). There will come a day when we will depart from this mortal life on earth and transition into a place of immortal/eternal life. Where that place ends up being is part conscious choice and part subconscious directive.

There are only two destinations available for eternal life. One is hell and the other is heaven. Which one do you prefer? Like any other journey, planning is an important part of assuring you reach your desired destination. The time to plan and prepare for departure, travel/transition, and arrival is *before* your actual departure. The same thing holds true for your eternal departure.

Eternity is the future for us all, and destination heaven is the desire of every born-again believer.

How to Invest for Eternity

There are three ways to invest for Divine eternity. They are:

1. God's Plan
2. God's Will
3. God's Purpose

God's plan is to reach people, touch, and change their lives with compassion through you and me. God's plan is for us to make a difference in people's lives and influence them for the Kingdom of Heaven. That should be our goal daily. Be alert to any opportunity that presents itself to share, encourage, and bless others. The best way to achieve this is to develop an eternity mindset, because every soul matters to God.

God's will is for us to obey His Word and do His will. Basically, God expects us to make ourselves available to Kingdom investment opportunities. He wants us to do something that impacts or influences someone else for Kingdom purpose.

God's purpose is to grow or increase the population of heaven. He does not want to lose or forfeit one soul. Second Peter addresses the fact that God wants everyone to come to repentance:

> Nevertheless, do not let this one fact escape you, beloved, that with the Lord one day is as a thousand years and a thousand years as one day. The Lord does not delay and is not tardy or slow about what He promises, according to some people's conception of slowness, but He is long-suffering (extraordinarily patient) toward you, not desiring that any should perish, but that all should turn to repentance. But the day of the Lord will come like a thief, and then the heavens will vanish (pass away) with a thunderous crash, and the [material] elements [of the universe] will be dissolved with fire, and the earth and the works that are upon it will be burned up. Since all these things are thus in the process of being dissolved, what kind of person ought [each of] you to be [in the meanwhile] in consecrated and holy behavior and devout and godly qualities.
> —2 Peter 3:8–11 AMPC

In the meantime, God needs us to be His hands, feet, and voice on earth to help grow the population of heaven. And in so doing, we qualify for our names to be written in the Book of Life (Heaven's Registry).

Divine Destiny

God wants your name in the Book of Life! And the only way to get it there is to follow His plan, be in His will, and fulfill His purpose for your life. He created you on purpose, for His Kingdom purpose! And He needs us (you and me) to be willing to follow His plan. That is the *only* way to get our names in the Lamb's Book of Life. Just being saved, born again, and having accepted Jesus as our Lord and Savior does not fully qualify and guarantee us to spend eternity with Him. It is the *beginning* of qualification.

To fulfill God's plan, will, and purpose for our lives—and to qualify for eternity with Jesus—requires a mindset of eternal life! So what is a mindset? A mindset is a fixed mental attitude or disposition that predetermines a person's response to and interpretation of a situation or event.[2]

God wants you to help populate heaven with someone else other than yourself. He expects you to connect with and care about others. This is something that should come naturally, since we are created in the image of God (in His likeness), we have His spirit, we are His children, we have His love within us, and we have the mind of Christ . . . but it is not that way. It does not happen automatically. We have to choose to make it happen. We have to do this on purpose. We must give thought to what we can do and how we can do it. We have to develop an eternity mindset by using the information and techniques that are covered in this book.

God wants you to influence others for eternity with Jesus Christ. Use your influence to impact someone's life. This can be done one on one or through a group, organizational, or ministry involvement that reaches, touches, and changes lives with the love of God and the Gospel of Jesus Christ. You don't have to preach to them. Just love them, show interest in them, and demonstrate you care about them. When you develop this mindset, opportunities will open up to you. I encourage you to make a decision to invest in their eternity!

Three Types of Investment

There are three types of investment in eternity:

1. Time (Energy and Effort)
2. Talent (Skills and Services)
3. Treasure (Money and Material Possessions)

All three of these are what God gives to you. What you do with them is what you give back to Him! Let's consider each one.

Time: The Most Valuable Resource

Time is the most precious thing in the world. This is true not only because time that has passed can never be retrieved but also because time, wisely and diligently employed, can bring practically everything else that is worthwhile in the world.

Each of us has all the time there is! One of the most interesting characteristics of time is that it plays no favorites in its distribution. Neither the wealthy nor influential can monopolize it. We all have it in an absolutely equal quantity. Every one of us has the same allocation of time in our lifetime. That lifetime allocation is divided into units of time. There are sixty seconds in every minute, sixty minutes in every hour, and twenty-four hours in every day. We can do whatever we want to with the time we have been given, but we will be held accountable to God for how we employ His precious gift of time.

God has given everyone twenty-four hours a day. A good application of that time can develop opportunities to serve others and a chance to lay up rich rewards for the life to come. The reward or return from investing one's time in service for Kingdom purpose is extremely high. A wise application of time can result in material things, wealth, health, relationships, character, success, advancement, growth, and a more abundant knowledge of God and His will for your life.

If we were to evaluate the overall activities of the average church member at large, we would find that most are not essential, productive, or profitable.

The book of Ecclesiastes reminds us of the significance of applied time:

> For everything there is a season, and a time for every purpose under heaven.
> —Ecclesiastes 3:1 ASV

The best way to find the time for everything is to better manage your time for a successful investment. We need to be faithful stewards of our time, talent, and treasure. Each one of us has all the time we need to do everything God would have us to do. If we will seek God and ask for guidance and direction in how to employ our time, He is faithful to provide to us exactly what we need. Everyone can find an area of Christian service to get involved in and invest their time. That would put a smile on God's face.

Talent: Everyone Can Do Something

Everyone can do something because everyone has talents. God has a definite purpose for the life of every individual. He created each of us on purpose, and if anyone says he or she cannot serve God because they lack ability, by default, they deny that God created them. God has not failed to provide us with the talents and resources needed to accomplish our purpose. However, if you don't know what your purpose in life is, then you have nothing to inspire you. There is a saying that goes like this: "If you aim at nothing, you are sure to hit it every time."

That is not God's will. He has endowed us with talents, skills, and abilities according to the plans He has for us. God has a need for every Christian believer to employ their talents, no matter how great or small the talent. Everyone can do something, and that is how we cooperate in His service.

Every human being will give account of himself to God according to Romans 14:12 and 1 Peter 4:5. This judgment and, hopefully, the rewards, are on an individual basis. We shall be rewarded in eternity for what we do in this life on earth.

Someone with what may be considered small talents who makes use of them faithfully in the Lord's service will receive the same reward from the Lord on that day of judgment as the faithful servant who has received twice as great a number of talents and a higher level of skills! It does not matter what title, position, reputation, or status that someone may have on earth. Everyone is judged the same in eternity!

The key to faithful stewardship of God-given talents is in our love for God and our desire to please Him, obey His Word, and do His will. Churches are full of people who have not yet become stewards of their talents. The unused abilities and misapplied skills within the church saddens God's heart. You need to discover your talents and put them to use for Kingdom purpose. God has given you your individual and specific talents to fulfill the mission He has for you. It is up to you to discover what those talents are and to do your part to develop and employ them.

The Word of God is pretty explicit on putting to use our God-given talents in His service. Here are a few applicable scriptures as written by Paul the Apostle.

Not All Are Given the Same Gifts

> For I wish that all men were even as I myself. But each one has his own gift from God, one in this manner and another in that.
> —1 Corinthians 7:7 NKJV

> For as we have many members in one body, but all the members do not have the same function, so we being many, are one body in Christ, and individually members of one another. Having then gifts differing according to the grace that is given to us, let us use them.
> —Romans 12:4-6

> There are diversities of gifts, but the same Spirit. . . . But one and the same Spirit works all these things, distributing to each one individually as He wills.
> —1 Corinthians 12:4, 11

We Have an Obligation to Discover Our Talents

Once we discover our talents and gifts, we must employ them. Let me remind you to stir up the gift of God which is in you:

> Do not neglect the gift that is in you.
> —I Timothy 4:14

> Each of you should use whatever gift you have received to serve others, as faithful stewards of God's grace in its various forms.
> —1 Peter 4:10 NIV

This clearly describes what we are expected to do with our talents and gifts. This is God's expectation, and each one of us must give an account of our stewardship. There is no better way to stress the importance of this truth than by referencing the Word of God!

> So then every one of us will give account of himself to God.
> —Romans 14:12 KJV

When talents are put to use, they will increase. Our talents can be put to use every day. There are surely many opportunities for our talents to be released in our daily duties. It can be accomplished through our attitude toward our work, the manner in which we respond (instead of react) to a situation, and the way we interact with coworkers, customers, and managers.

We can accomplish Kingdom work by being a good steward of our time and talents when applied to worthwhile activities. I am sure many opportunities are overlooked and neglected every day.

Do not pass by or pass up small opportunities while waiting for large ones. The Lord is pleased with small things done well and done with a spirit of excellence and honor. God wants our best, and for all He has done for us, that is the least we should do for Him.

Treasure: Stewardship of Possessions

Some of the best financial advice you could receive is to lay up treasures in heaven. For the Christian, it is a priority investment. This section is not going to address tithing and the act of giving as much as the heart of the matter. The stewardship of money and possessions is a very important topic for God and ranks near the top of His list of lessons He wants us to learn and apply. This is evidenced in the fact that more is written in the New Testament regarding the stewardship of money or possessions than any other single subject. In fact, sixteen of Jesus's thirty-eight parables, which is 42 percent of them, deal with possessions.[3] One out of ten verses in Matthew, Mark, and Luke addresses the righteous management of material wealth.[4]

The KJV Bible refers to "pray" or "prayer" 547 times; to faith, 336 times; and to money and material possessions more than 2,000 times![5] Seems like God did not intend for us to treat the subject of money and possessions lightly. This is definitely something that we need to be mindful of. Do you think God would have given such great emphasis to this matter if it were not of utmost importance? God is more interested in our heart rather than our treasure.

> Do not lay up for yourselves treasures on earth, where moth and rust destroy and where thieves

> break in and steal; but lay up for yourselves treasures in heaven, where neither moth nor rust destroys and where thieves do not break in and steal. For where your treasure is there your heart will be also.
> —Matthew 6:19-21 NKJV

Now since we have determined that one's heart and mind occupy the same space, then where your treasure is, there your mind will be also. Our thoughts about money and possessions will drive our actions where and when money and possessions are involved. If your heart is on the altar, your money will be there also. The study of human nature reveals the fact that the sincerity and commitment of a person's interest in something is indicated by the way they put money into it.

The investment of money in worldly concerns reflects a person's true interest. A person's attitude toward the production of money, the accumulation of money, the saving of money, the investment of money, the spending and distribution of money, and the giving of money uncovers the character of the person. The most telling attitude and character of a person is revealed through giving. A person's heart and mind becomes transparent in the act of giving or not giving. There is a level of knowledge and mature understanding that accompanies both tithing and giving.

A member of the church who contributes to the church budget definitely has a share in the preaching of the gospel and the work of the various ministries. A supporter of the church or ministry budget helps provide the necessary finances for its productive and effective operations.

There is no better way to invest money with so many useful and far-reaching benefits than in Kingdom works. No other investment can deliver such a large magnitude of satisfaction on earth and rich rewards in heaven. It is by far the best investment with the best return in this life and the life hereafter.

There is a standard for giving that is laid out in scripture in the New Testament. Giving is the key to open the channels of supply and provision in your life, and God is Jehovah-Jire . . . the God who supplies all your needs! Let's briefly examine a few:

1. Giving is an essential acknowledgement of our indebtedness to God.

> Freely you have received; freely give.
> —Matthew 10:8 NIV

2. Giving is better that receiving.

   You should remember the words of the Lord Jesus Himself said:

> It is more blessed to give than to receive.
> —Acts 20:35

3. Giving should be cheerful and should be motivated by love rather than required by law.

> Each of you should give what you have decided in your heart to give, not reluctantly or under compulsion, for God loves a cheerful giver.
> —2 Corinthians 9:7

4. Giving should be generous.

> For if you give, you will get! Your gift will return to you in full and overflowing measure, pressed down, shaken together to make room for more, and running over. Whatever measure you use to give—large or small—will be used to measure what is given back to you.
> —Luke 6:38 TLB

5. Giving should be proportionate. God expects all of us to give to support His work, and He has given a mandate regarding the gift.

> Each of you must bring a gift in proportion to the way the Lord your God has blessed you.
> —Deuteronomy 16:17 NIV

> Every man shall give as he is able, according to the blessing of the Lord your God which He has given you.
> —Deuteronomy 16:17 NKJV

God needs men and women who are faithful with possessions. He knows that if you are faithful with little, He can trust you with much more.

As we invest of our treasure to support God's cause in the earth, the Lord makes it possible for each one of us to lay up eternal treasures in heaven for eternity. That is exciting!

Consider the following:

> Tell those who are rich not to be proud and not to trust in their money, which will soon be gone, but their pride and trust should be in the living God who always richly gives us all we need for our enjoyment. Tell them to use their money to do good. They should be rich in good works and should give happily to those in need, always being ready to share with others whatever God has given them. By doing this they will be storing up real treasure for themselves in heaven . . . it is the only safe investment for eternity! And they will be living a fruitful Christian life down here as well.
> —1 Timothy 6:17-19 TLB

God is aware and takes notice of all the gifts made by His children today, whether those gifts be large or small, and He rewards them accordingly.

Our usefulness and happiness in this world and our joys and rewards in heaven throughout the endless eternity will be in proportion to our faithfulness as stewards here on earth in the use of all the talents and resources with which God has entrusted to us.

Our Heavenly Father is all-wise, just, and righteous. He assures that faithful men and women, who invest their time, talent, and treasure, as well as other resources in extending the Kingdom, shall share equally with the missionaries, evangelists, and other workers who minister to needy humanity in the name of our Savior Jesus Christ.

A faithful steward of all the resources which God has given him enjoys a good conscience, a sense of God's approval here on earth, and a share in extending Christ's Kingdom out to the ends of the earth. A faithful steward lays up for himself eternal dividends and rewards in heaven.

Droughts, famines, wars, tornados, hurricanes, and other calamities can wipeout legitimate lifesavings in a moment's time, but the investment we have made in heaven, through the contributions of our possessions and our service in the Kingdom of God, are untouchable by the Devil and any economic afflictions here on earth. Our investments in stewardship are deposited by our Lord, for us, in the Eternal Bank of Heaven. There is no force in all the universe that can rob us of them, nor can any evil force intercept or interrupt the constant flow of the generous and gracious dividends that only God supplies.

Anyone who sets their mind to support the local church budget to help maintain the church equipment and carry forward the preaching, teaching, healing, deliverance, and helping ministries of Jesus Christ is making the best investment in the world. No other financial investment has such diverse, useful, and far-reaching channels of impact for the Kingdom of Heaven. No other investment will deliver such satisfaction in this life and rich rewards in the life to come. It is by far and hands-down the best financial investment with the best return for a lifetime and beyond.

Let's review a few BCV (book, chapter, and verse) principles and standards for investing through giving and sharing:

1. Giving is an essential recognition and acknowledgement of our honor to God.

> Honor the Lord with your possessions.
> —Proverbs 3:9 NKJV

2. Giving is better than receiving.

> I have shown you in every way, by laboring like this, that you must support the weak. And remember the word of the Lord Jesus, that He said, "It is more blessed to give than to receive."
> —Acts 20:35

3. Giving should be cheerful and prompted by love rather than driven by law.

> Let each one [give] as he has made up his own mind and purposed in his heart, not reluctantly or sorrowfully or under compulsion, for God loves (He takes pleasure in, prizes above other things, and is unwilling to abandon or to do without) a cheerful (joyous,

> "prompt to do it") giver [whose heart is in his giving]. And God is able to make all grace (every favor and earthly blessing) come to you in abundance, so that you may always and under all circumstances and whatever the need be self-sufficient [possessing enough to require no aid or support and furnished in abundance for every good work and charitable donation]. As it is written, He [the benevolent person] scatters abroad; He gives to the poor; His deeds of justice and goodness and kindness and benevolence will go on and endure forever! And [God] Who provides seed to the sower and bread for eating will also provide and multiply your [resources for] sowing and increase the fruits of your righteousness [which manifest itself in active goodness, kindness, and charity].
>
> —2 Corinthians 9:7–10 AMPC

4. Giving should be generous.

> Give, and [gifts] will be given to you; good measure, pressed down, shaken together, and running over, will they pour into [the pouch formed by] the bosom [of your robe and used as a bag]. For with the measure you deal out [with the measure you use when you confer benefits on others], it will be measured back to you.
>
> —Luke 6:38

It is extremely encouraging to know that the Lord has made it possible for each of us to lay up eternal treasures in heaven while here on earth. For the believer, this gives purpose to prosperity and wealth, no matter on what level it is measured.

Ask Yourself this Question: Are You a Robber or a Thief?

> "Will a man rob God? Yet you are robbing Me! But you say, 'How have we robbed you?' In tithes and offerings. You are cursed with a curse, for you are robbing Me, the whole nation of you!"
> —Malachi 3:8-9 NASB

Are you robbing God? This should be an alarming accusation for any Christian. And verse 9 is extremely sobering, especially being stated by God! God is declaring a shocking truth that His people continue to rob Him by stealing from Him and cheating Him "of the tithes and offerings due to me." A quick assumption could be that God is referring to money. But please understand that there is a variety of ways we can rob God and abort or short-circuit our purpose in life in the process.

The truth is that we rob God whenever we do not give Him our "tithes and offerings." This is foundational to our relationship with Him. It is not an option!

Tithing is proof positive of our acknowledgement that everything we have is provided by God (Jehovah-Jireh). Tithing establishes our willingness to be obedient to God's Word and to do His will. It also demonstrates that we believe He can and *will* supply all our needs. When we maintain tithing as a priority, it unlocks the windows of heaven for us to receive an overflow of His blessings.

Now, regarding offerings, I submit to you that there are many kinds of "offerings." God looks at the broader perspective of our entire being, including our time, talent, and treasure. As a matter of fact, our whole life and everything in it can be an offering unto God. The concept of offerings was originated by God in His Word.

> You must present as the LORD's portion the best and holiest part of everything given to you.
> —Numbers 18:29 NIV

God has clearly expressed that He wants nothing less than our best in everything and of everything that we do and have. Keep God's principles about offerings on your mind every day of your life. Live by these principles and remember that God sees and knows everything you do and have, because He is the source of it all.

> Every good thing given and every perfect gift is from above, coming down from the Father of lights, with whom there is no variation or shifting shadow.
> —James 1:17 NASB

Let's take a prayer pause right here to thank God, our Heavenly Father:

Father God, we take this moment to give You thanks for the time, talent, and treasure that You have so graciously given to us. We dedicate them to you. Help us, Lord God, to give You our best in everything we do. In Jesus's Holy name. Amen.

As mentioned earlier, our usefulness and happiness on earth and our joys and rewards in heaven throughout eternity will be in proportion to our faithful stewardship here on earth in the employment of all the time, talent, and treasures which God has entrusted to us. May we never dishonor nor disappoint God, our Heavenly Father.

Programmed For Life Everlasting

Hopefully, by now, you understand the power and works of the subconscious mind. The assurance of eternal life with Jesus Christ is facilitated by a Divine Mind. It is to your benefit to develop an eternity mindset with an eternal perspective.

Let's review the definition of the term "mindset": It is a fixed mental attitude or disposition that predetermines a person's response to and interpretation of a situation or event.[6]

So, in light of this definition, an eternity mindset can be defined as a mental attitude or disposition that is fixed on eternal life and predetermines your response to and your interpretation of living for infinite time, which we call "forever." It includes your eternal destination (or where you will spend eternity) and how you will get there.

Your eternal destination is established, determined, and set by your thoughts, words, and deeds or actions . . . all of which will be reviewed and accounted for on Judgment Day.

> But I say to you that for every idle word men speak, they will give account of it in the day of judgment.
> —Matthew 12:36 NKJV

> And there is no creature hidden from His sight, but all things are naked and open to the eyes of Him to whom we must give account.
> —Hebrews 4:13

So, based on the Word of God, it becomes very clear that in order to secure your name in the Book of Life for eternity and reach your desired destiny, you need to begin by remembering your origin. Come to the place where you understand the relationship between your mind and the Holy Spirit.

CHAPTER 15:

Holy Spirit and the Mind

The relationship between the Holy Spirit and your mind can be described with two words: absolutely powerful! One of the biggest mistakes that Christians make is not even attempting to understand the work of a Divine Mind when connected to the infinite power of Holy Spirit.

Think for a moment of how God designed and created us in His likeness. We are made up of three parts: spirit, soul, and body. You may be wondering: where does the mind fit in with these three parts? First of all, a spirit is what you are. Soul is who you are. And body is where you are. Your mind is the primary element of your soul. We will cover more on that coming up just ahead.

The Apostle Paul wrote in scripture:

> Now may the God of peace himself sanctify you completely, and may your whole spirit and soul and body be kept blameless at the coming of our Lord Jesus Christ.
> —1 Thessalonians 5:23 ESV

Your body is the only physical or tangible part of your tripart being. Your body can be seen and touched. You are also made up of nonphysical or intangible aspects which include your soul, spirit, intellect, will, emotions, mind (conscious and subconscious), etc. These intangible aspects really exist and make up the whole you. Your body is the physical or tangible host for the soul and spirit, which are the prime nonphysical or intangible aspects of your tripart being.

Your soul represents the character and personality of your being. Your soul lives in your body. In Genesis, it is written:

> And the Lord God formed man in the dust of the ground, and breathed into his nostrils the breath of life; and man became a living soul.
> —Genesis 2:7 KJV

Your soul consists of your mind/intellect (which includes your conscious, subconscious, and unconscious), plus your will and your emotions. Your mind and your spirit are harmoniously connected to form what scriptures regard as your heart. And your heart is the control center for your will and emotions.

<u>Your spirit</u> is of God's class and in God's image. Man is a spirit, created to be the associate and companion of God, our Creator. God does not exist for our purpose. We exist for *His* purpose. God created you and me to fulfill His plan, will, and purpose on earth.

In the process of His purpose, only God has the inventory to provide a new heart and new spirit.

> A new heart will I give you and a new spirit will I put within you . . . And I will put <u>My Spirit</u> within you and

> cause you to walk in My statutes, and you shall heed My ordinances and do them.
> —Ezekiel 36:26-27 AMPC

God can give you a new heart and a new spirit. Once He puts His Spirit within you; you will no longer be moved to follow mere human nature or the earthly nature of man apart from divine influence, and therefore prone to sin and opposed to God. Our spirit man is subject to daily renewal. And because of that, we do not lose heart or become discouraged.

> For this reason we never become discouraged. Even though our physical being is gradually decaying, yet our spiritual being is renewed day after day.
> —2 Corinthians 4:16 GNT

There is no procedure we need to perform. We simply make ourselves available and receptive, and the Spirit of God does its work.

By now you should realize that spirit and soul are two separate things. Working together, they generate power with personality. To support this premise of the separation between soul and spirit, I present to you Hebrews:

> For the word of God is living and powerful, and sharper than any two-edged sword, piercing even to the division of soul and spirit, and of joints and marrow, and is a discerner of the thoughts and intents of the heart.
> —Hebrews 4:12 NKJV

Now that we have addressed the three parts of man as spirit, soul, and body, I want to summarize with a description of their very specific functions. Each part has its very own individual function as follows:

- The body contacts and operates in the physical and material realm.
- The soul contacts and operates in the intellectual realm.
- The spirit contacts and operates in the spiritual realm.

It is the spirit of man that knows God. But that is only if a man is open, available, and receptive to receive His Spirit. We have the option to reject God's Spirit. If we are open and receptive, and desire to receive the Spirit of God and be His host, then we have the same spirit—the Holy Spirit—within us! You see, the Holy Spirit *is* God!

A mind without the Holy Spirit is like a day without sunshine. A mind without the Holy Spirit is impossible to be a Divine Mind! Therefore, the Holy Spirit not only needs to be on your mind (conscious mind), but He also needs to be in your mind (subconscious mind). Your unconscious mind is your direct connection to the Ultimate and Infinite Source of everything good and perfect: God Himself. So how does God get His thoughts, His promises, and His Word to you? By way of the Holy Spirit, who God has given access to your subconscious mind. Thank You, Holy Spirit, for being God's messenger and our helper.

Why is this so vital? Because without the Holy Spirit indwelling the mind, one cannot truly be a child of God. In an effort to validate this point and to drive home the truth while giving more insight for your thoughts to sincerely consider the connection between Holy Spirit and your mind, let's review a few scriptures from the books of Romans and Timothy.

> So that the righteous and just requirement of the Law might be fully met in us who live and move not in the ways of the flesh but in the ways of the Spirit [our

lives governed not by the standards and according to the dictates of the flesh, but controlled by the Holy Spirit]. For those who are according to the flesh and are controlled by its unholy desires set their minds on and pursue those things which gratify the flesh, but those who are according to the Spirit and are controlled by the desires of the Spirit set their minds on and seek those things which gratify the [Holy] Spirit. Now the mind of the flesh [which is sense and reason without Holy Spirit] is death [death that comprises all the miseries arising from sin, both here and hereafter]. But the mind of the [Holy] Spirit is life and [soul] peace [both now and forever]. [That is] because the mind of the flesh [with its carnal thoughts and purposes] is hostile to God, for it does not submit itself to God's Law; indeed it cannot. So then those who are living the life of the flesh [catering to the appetites and impulses of their carnal nature] cannot please or satisfy God, or be acceptable to Him. But you are not living the life of the flesh, you are living the life of the Spirit, if the [Holy] Spirit of God [really] dwells within you [directs and controls you]. But if anyone does not possess the [Holy] Spirit of Christ, he is none of His [he does not belong to Christ, is not truly a child of God]. . . . For all who are led by the Spirit of God are sons of God. . . . The Spirit Himself [thus] testifies together with our own spirit, [assuring us] that we are children of God.
—Romans 8:4-9, 14, 16 AMPC

Through the power of the Holy Spirit who lives within us, carefully guard the precious truth that has been entrusted to you.
—2 Timothy 1:14 NLT

Your walk on the path to eternity must be led by the Spirit of God. The Holy Spirit must indwell your mind, and you must move and follow His guide. So how do you get to heaven without the Holy Spirit indwelling your mind? The answer is . . . you *cannot*!

A Divine Mind is a mind that is indwelled by and cooperates with Holy Spirit. Without performing the activities required to develop a Divine Mind, we fall woefully short of our status as a child of God. We must do our part to qualify. It is well worth the effort because the alternative is not pretty or appealing at all. Invest in eternity. You will receive the best return on investment here on earth and in heaven.

If you want to give yourself the best opportunity for your name to be in the Book of Life and to hear the words, "Well done, good and faithful servant" (see Matthew 25:21), consider employing your subconscious mind and set your heart to develop a Divine Mind.

There are three primary elements to be managed and controlled for developing a Divine Mind and setting your posture for eternal life with Jesus Christ. They are:

1. Your Thoughts
2. Your Words
3. Your Actions

Remember, what you think about most expands in your life. Thoughts are seeds, and thoughts create results. Words have power. And actions speak louder than words. This means your words are amplified by your actions; therefore, your words become even more powerful. Another way of looking at this is that when corresponding actions are mixed with words of faith, then maximum power is released. Let your actions be in cooperation with your words so they don't cancel each other out.

Let's visit a couple of scriptures to help put these comments into proper perspective.

1. **Thoughts**: What you think about most becomes reality and expands in your life.

> For as he thinks in his heart, so is he.
> —Proverbs 23:7 NKJV

God knows your thoughts!

> O Lord, you have examined my heart and know everything about me. You know when I sit or stand. When far away You know my every thought. You know what I am going to say before I even say it.
> —Psalm 139:1-3, 4 TLB

*****

What if Jesus could hear your every thought? Would you be inclined to maybe change the way you think and control your thoughts? Well, Jesus does hear your thoughts. So like Father, like Son.

> But Jesus, knowing their thoughts, said, "Why do you think evil in your hearts?"
> —Matthew 9:4 NKJV

The fact that Jesus asked this question demonstrates that He examines our thoughts and motives. Are there wrong thoughts that you tend to give attention or consideration to? What are some thoughts that you have allowed to gain influence in your mind and heart? We must practice taking every thought captive that is not pleasing to God.

> For the weapons of our warfare are not carnal but mighty in God for pulling down strongholds, casting down arguments and every high thing that exalts itself against the knowledge of God, bringing every thought into captivity to the obedience of Christ.
> —2 Corinthians 10:4-5

2. **Words**: God hears and knows your thoughts, but He most often responds to your words, because your words reflect what is in your heart. Pay attention to Luke 6:45:

> A good man out of the good treasure of his heart brings forth good; and an evil man out of the evil treasure of his heart brings forth evil. <u>For out of the abundance of the heart his mouth speaks</u>.
> —Luke 6:45

*****

Our good words will get God's attention. See what God did for Daniel:

> Then he said to me, "Do not fear, Daniel, for from the first day that <u>you set your heart to understand</u>, and to <u>humble yourself</u> before your God, your words were heard; and <u>I have come because of your words</u>.
> —Daniel 10:12

> Then he continued, "Do not be afraid, Daniel. Since the first day that you set your mind to gain understanding and to humble yourself before your God, your words were heard, and I have come in response to them.
> —Daniel 10:12 NIV

Comparing these two translations of Daniel 10:12, we again confirm that the mind and the heart occupy the same space and are referred to interchangeably. Even scriptures acknowledge that a hardened heart represents or is the same as a closed mind. As we can see, at the end of the verse, the angel responds to the words of Daniel. This is a type and shadow of how God responds to our words, when we set our "heart/mind." This all comes full circle, because the way you set your heart and mind is with your words. Let your lips declare what the Word of God says about you. Be deliberate and intentional with your words and speak or declare on purpose. In Isaiah 57:19, God says that "I create the fruit of the lips." He is the source of the creative power of your words.

We need to remain mindful of our words because scripture tells us in Matthew that

> For by your words you will be justified, and by your words you will be condemned.
> —Matthew 12:37 NASB

3. **Actions**: Faith and words of faith are important; however, faith without works or corresponding action is unfruitful and dead. In other words, it produces no results. You see, faith is considered to be a verb in the English language. A verb is a word that describes some form of action or activity. To expect faith to work without you doing something is deceiving yourself. Take a look at the BCV (book, chapter, and verse) below.

> But be doers of the Word, and not hearers only, deceiving yourselves.
> —James 1:22 NKJV

What this means is that if you just listen to the Word and don't obey, you are like a man looking at his face in a mirror.

As soon as he walks away, he cannot see himself anymore or does not remember what he looks like. You see, the mirror represents the conscious mind with God's Word. If anyone keeps looking steadily into God's Word, he will not only remember it, but he will also do what it says, because it gets locked down into his subconscious mind. This creates the reality, and God will greatly bless you in everything you do.

So why is it crucial to invest the time and take the actions to set your heart and mind? Well, Matthew 12:34 tells us that a man's heart determines his speech. For out of the abundance or overflow of the heart the mouth speaks. The twelfth chapter of Matthew goes on to tell us that a good person's speech reveals the rich treasuries within them. An evil-hearted person is filled with venom, and their speech reveals it. And I tell you this, we all must give account on Judgment Day for every idle word we speak. Your words now drive your fate, because either you will be justified by them or you will be condemned by them.

The following verses will shed more light and give us more insight into the answer.

> A good man brings good things out of the good stored up in his heart, and an evil man brings evil things out of the evil stored up in his heart. For the mouth speaks what the heart is full of.
> —Luke 6:45 NIV

> You brood of vipers, how can you, being evil, speak what is good? For the mouth speaks out of that which fills the heart.
> —Matthew 12:34 NASB

> A good person produces good things from the treasury of a good heart, and an evil person produces evil things from the treasury of an evil heart.
> —Matthew 12:35 NLT

> But those things which proceed out of the mouth come from the heart, and they defile a man. For out of the heart proceed evil thoughts.
> —Matthew 15:18 NKJV

I encourage you and challenge you to *program* your mind and heart so that the above scriptures will be truly applicable, active, and operative in your life.

CHAPTER 16:

How to Develop a Divine Mind

The process necessary to develop a Divine Mind are laid out in scriptures as presented on previous pages of this book. Please allow me to provide two verses of scripture that support the development process with guidance on what to think, when to think, and why to think.

Positive thinking yields positive results, and negative thinking yields negative results. You have the power of choice at your disposal. Choose wisely.

Philippians instructs on what to think:

> Finally, believers, whatever is true, whatever is honorable and worthy of respect, whatever is right and confirmed by God's word, whatever is pure and wholesome, whatever is lovely and brings peace, whatever is admirable and of good repute; if there is any excellence, if there is anything worthy of praise, think continually on these things [center your mind on them, and implant them in your heart].
> —Philippians 4:8 AMP

Joshua instructs on when and why to think:

> This Book of the Law shall not depart from your mouth, but you shall read [and meditate on] it day and night, so that you may be careful to do [everything] in accordance with all that is written in it; for then you will make your way prosperous, and then you will be successful.
> —Joshua 1:8

Please understand that your mind is the master controller of your present and future, your success and failure, your sickness and health, and your abundance and lack.

Your Divine Mind functions as your life's spiritual positioning system (SPS) and lane detection sensors, all working together to give you directions, instructions, and navigation monitoring, including any course corrections needed to reach your goals along the way to your final destination. Remember that it is operative 24-7-365. Trust it, rely on it, and follow it!

The most important activity you can perform is to program your subconscious and develop a Divine Mind. It is the link to success in life on earth and in heaven. Consequently, a Divine Mind is your *most valuable asset*! Invest in it.

To develop a Divine Mind requires an investment of dedicated time, focused effort, and unwavering commitment. Success in life through Jesus Christ is available to each one of us. Where is it found? In your mind and mouth, according to Joshua 1:8. Do you want to be more successful in life . . . spiritually, mentally, physically, socially, emotionally, and financially? If you have been looking for the secret of true success, this is it! Renew your mind, fill your heart, and engage your mouth to speak declarations in accordance with God's Word. God has equipped you to fulfill His plan, will, and purpose for your life through your thoughts, words, and deeds (an action that is performed intentionally or consciously).

The act of programming your subconscious mind and transforming it into a Divine Mind that will help secure your desired destination for eternity (in heaven) as well as success here on earth is established and set in place by your thoughts, words, and deeds. Invest time and energy in programming your Divine Mind with the Word and promises of God. Also include your goals and desires.

Begin to program your life on purpose, for His purpose, and build rewards on earth and in heaven!

You can confidently achieve success in life with the mind of Christ.

CHAPTER 17:

The Unconscious Mind Connection

Up to now we have covered little bit about the conscious mind and an extensive amount about the subconscious mind. Now it is time to take a closer look into the unconscious mind. So buckle your seat belt, because we are getting ready to delve a little deeper into the works of a Divine Mind.

The conscious, subconscious, and the unconscious all work together to create our reality in a powerful way. If you think of the mind as a pyramid, then the following illustration may help you understand how they all work together, like a three-legged stool. A three-legged stool cannot stand on its own, on one or two legs. It requires all three legs to stand on its own.

Three Sections of a Pyramid
Three Parts of the Mind

A pyramid has three sections, and so does the mind. The top section of the pyramid is the apex, the middle section is the core, and the bottom section is the base. The size of each section of the pyramid illustrates the relative percentage of the workload for each of the three sections of the mind. The apex represents the conscious mind, with 5 percent of the total workload of the mind. The core represents the subconscious mind, with 95 percent of the total workload, and the base represents the unconscious mind, with an infinite proportion of the total workload of the mind.

The unconscious mind is the infinite (∞) and totally unlimited part of the mind. The unconscious mind consists of the processes, functions, and operations that occur automatically, without awareness by the conscious and subconscious parts of the mind.[1] Thus, the unconscious mind is not available for introspection and includes thoughts, processes, memories, interests, instincts, motivations, intentions, and more, as it is directly connected to the Divine source of Infinite Intelligence.

Also, for a Divine Mind, the Spirit of God and the awareness of God is in the subconscious part of the mind, along with faith, hope, love, righteousness, and beliefs. The spiritual connection with God resides and takes place in the unconscious part of the human mind. The spiritual nature, communications, and the operations of the unconscious mind is what I want to focus on briefly in this section.

The one word that describes the difference between the three parts of mind is the word "awareness." The conscious mind always operates in awareness. The subconscious mind operates in an "awareness on demand" or in an "as needed" mode. And the unconscious mind always operates in total unawareness by the conscious mind. You could say that the unconscious mind operates deep undercover. It is the stealth member of the tripartite mind. God and His Spirit dwell and operate in you, in the space of your subconscious and unconscious mind. This is what upgrades your human mind to a Divine Mind. Remember the definition of "divine"? Anything that is of, from, or by God. When you have the mind of Christ, you are directly connected to God, your Heavenly Father, just as Jesus was when He walked the earth as a man.

The Purpose and Role of the Unconscious Mind

God designed the human mind the way He did on purpose . . . *for* a purpose. The unconscious mind is the true controlling element in our lives. Now, that can be negative or positive, depending on what spirit is hosted there. One can be led in a good way or a bad way, without our conscious or subconscious awareness. It is like being on autopilot that is connected to GPS or a PGNCS (primary guidance, navigation, and control system) that we spoke of earlier. We are being led by whatever spirit is within our unconscious mind.

This is important to understand, because an unconscious thought is what drives and determines our words, our actions, our behavior, emotions, our attitudes, personality, and character . . . essentially, the "core" of who we are. Our identity and who we are is determined by the unconscious. This is where our human spirit resides. This is the deepest part of our existence.[2] It is also the pathway of dreams and visions. Our unconscious mind is the spiritual connection to God. The subconscious is where the heart is. So the communication interface between the unconscious and the subconscious will govern who you really are. As stated before, "As a man thinks in his heart, so is he."

For a Christian, the unconscious mind is the portal where the Spirit of God is received and transferred to the subconscious mind. God in us, the Hope of Glory, is established in the subconscious mind via the unconscious mind portal. If you are led by the Spirit, that leading comes from the unconscious mind, because that is where your spiritual communication originates for the believer. The power to believe is within your subconscious mind. Believe in the power of your Divine Mind!

Now understanding these basic truths about the way God intentionally designed the human mind gives you a blueprint for your success in life with the mind of Christ, which you have access to through your unconscious mind. If the blueprint you have been following in your life has not produced or has not gotten you to where you want to be, you might want to follow a new blueprint. For a Divine Mind, this book is it!!

It Is *All* in Your Mind

God loves you and wants to live in you. He wants to fill you with His Spirit. God is love and he wants a love relationship with you. Jesus even stated the first commandment in part as: "You shall love the Lord your God with all your heart . . . and with all your mind" (Matt. 22:37; Mark 12:30 NLV).

Think back to a person you have had a romantic love relationship with. You probably thought about them daily, maybe multiple times each day. You could not wait to spend time with them. And when you did get to spend time with them, it seemed like time stood still. You might have written them love letters or little love notes.

What have you done lately to express your love for God? Your love for God is in your mind and heart. Don't miss any opportunity to express or show that love in your personal way. He longs for that love relationship with you, and you have to be intentional in the relationship

How does God draw all men unto Himself? When you are born again, you become a new creature in your spirit, which is connected to your unconscious mind. God is Spirit and He created you in His image, as a spirit. That spirit is within your subconscious mind. When your subconscious mind connects with your unconscious mind, then your human spirit connects to the Spirit of God, and a transformation process takes place. And that will create a born-again experience.

The realization of your born-again status enters your unconscious from the Spirit of God and is transmitted to your subconscious where you can then be aware of it and be transformed. Then you become fully conscious of your deliverance and salvation. Praise God!

Here are just a few of the many characteristics of the Three Parts of Mind:

1. Conscious Mind—[Limited]
   - ∞ Limited belief; logic; analytical; educated mind; willpower; short-term memory; habits; self-esteem, critical thinking

2. Subconscious Mind - [Unlimited]
   - ∞ Insight; All thoughts, feelings, experiences stored here; programmed by your thoughts and words 24/7; intuition; imaginative; inner peace; lightning fast; mental imagery; incredibly powerful; creative, gut feelings; self-healing; inventive; wise; permanent memory storage

3. Unconscious Mind – [Infinite]
   - ∞ Spiritual connection; deepest part of existence; highest self; the core of who you are; drives the dreaming state; primal instinct; connected to Infinite Intelligence; mind of Christ

There is a Higher Presence/Infinite Intelligence present everywhere at all times (God). As we are born-again believers, God has full access to our unconscious mind. We have the mind of Christ, which is directly connected to God, i.e., the Wisdom and Spirit of God.

> "For my thoughts are not your thoughts, neither are your ways my ways," declares the Lord. "As the

> heavens are higher than the earth, so are my ways higher than your ways and my thoughts than your thoughts."
> —Isaiah 55:8-9 NIV

The connection between your unconscious mind and God (the source of Infinite Intelligence) takes the limits off of your mind. Once that connection is made, your unconscious mind becomes infinite. The only limits on your mind are the ones you put on it or you allow to be put on it, at the subconscious level.

In case you missed it, the Infinite Intelligence I speak of is actually the only source of Divine Intelligence, which is God Almighty. God can use Holy Spirit to get the broad spectrum of "information" into the subconscious mind.

Your conscious mind and your subconscious mind, on their own, is not directly connected to God. The subconscious mind is a transfer connection and can use the programmed information from this Divine source, but the subconscious mind cannot directly access the information. The information from this Divine source must be delivered to the subconscious mind. Once the subconscious mind receives the information, it can be bought into your conscious awareness. This is the creative process that takes place.

For a better understanding, I want to explain how the creative process works in a little more detail.

When you have a goal, a problem, or a specific desire, you can use techniques discussed earlier for programming your subconscious mind. Then your subconscious mind taps into the power of Infinite Intelligence and receives the answer, solution, or information. Once it is received into the subconscious mind, the subconscious mind presents the answer, solution, or information needed to your conscious mind to create awareness. This may happen suddenly, like a newsflash, or it may happen gradually over a period of time. You may even have to repeat the programming process by sowing the thought seed for your need. Once the answer, solution, or information gets to your conscious awareness, you must take appropriate actions.

Jesus lives in you. Christ in you is your only hope of glory. Make your heart and mind the host home of Jesus. Christ presence in your heart and mind cultivates the hope of all things working together for your good. And it gives you peace that passes all the understanding in your conscious mind. Hope and peace can work behind the scenes of the things you can see. The confidence of Jesus living inside of you (your mind and heart) every moment of your life will be projected as a light that others cannot help but notice.

What you are learning from this book right now can totally change the trajectory of your life and purpose if you will adopt and adapt. If you want to affect a change in your life at the core level, then you need a blueprint to follow that will not fail (see chapter 20).

CHAPTER 18:

Prayer of Acceptance and Salvation

Jesus loves you! He desires to have a relationship with you and to give you a life full of joy and purpose. If you don't know Jesus as your personal Lord and Savior, I would like for you to take this opportunity to meet Him. He is the truest *friend* you will ever have or need.

When we accept Jesus as our Lord and Savior and ask him to come into our heart, what we are really saying is this:

> Thank you, Jesus, for dying on the cross for me and forgiving my sins. Come into my heart. Forgive me of all my sins. Take control of my mind and my life. Make me a new person in You, right now. I believe that You are the Son of God and that You died on the cross for me. Help me to realize and know that I am saved and born again. Fill me with your Holy Spirit. Help me to do Your will and obey Your word all the days of my life. I accept and receive You as my Savior and my Lord.

That is what you are saying. So have you ever spoken words like that? I ask that question for three reasons:

1. If you have never prayed a prayer like that, you should!
2. If you have already prayed a prayer like that, but you have not experienced the difference you expected or hoped for. Or you prayed, but time and distance have come between you and Jesus. You're not as close as you once were . . . you should pray it again!
3. If you just want to refresh your relationship with Jesus and ask Him to renew your mind and your heart, you should recommit your life for a fresh start! So if you acknowledge any one of these three conditions, I want you to boldly speak the words of that prayer out loud. Read it again out loud, right now. Do it right now! This is the right place. This is the right day. This is the right time. Hallelujah. Thank you Lord Jesus. Read it now.

If you prayed the above prayer, I want to congratulate you and welcome you into the family of God. We are all His children, and He is our Heavenly Father. May God richly bless you. Now go find a church to join and become a member. Grow and serve.

CHAPTER 19:

Prayer for a Divine Mind

Salvation is the most precious gift from God through Jesus Christ. The second most precious and powerful gift from God is that of a Divine Mind. It is the primary gear that drives every area of your life.

I want to pray for you and your Divine Mind right now. I have included a prayer that you can use to pray for yourself. It also includes a few declarations in the prayer. Even though there are words provided for this prayer, once you apply your voiceprint and speak the words, they become your words and carry the power to not return to you void or empty but to accomplish what you have spoken. So pray with confidence.

> Oh God, my Heavenly Father . . . I come to You right now, believing for a Divine Mind. I thank you that I have the mind of Christ, and I hold the thoughts, feelings, and purpose of His heart. The Holy Spirit gives direction to my spirit and illumination to my mind. He leads me in the way I should go in all the

affairs of my life. He leads me by an inward witness through my subconscious mind. I place myself at Your disposal. The eyes of my understanding are being enlightened through my conscious mind. I trust in the Lord with all my heart and lean not to my own understanding. In all my ways, I acknowledge You, and You direct my paths. My mind plans my way, but the Lord directs my steps and makes them sure. My Divine Mind will educate, train, and develop my human spirit. In the name of Jesus, I am determined to take control of my tongue. I am thankful that the ability of God is released within me by the words of my mouth and the Word of God. Lord, help me to tame my temper and my tongue; I pray for a godly attitude. Father God, I pray that You take charge of and control my mind, channel my thoughts, guard my mouth, and guide my heart to fulfill Your plan, will, and purpose for my life. I declare that I am equipped to do the will of God. My mind is willing and my heart is obedient. Blessed be the name of the Lord God Almighty. Amen.

Closing Thought

The following is an excerpt from the book *Switch on Your Brain* by Dr. Caroline Leaf. In her book, she makes a statement that addresses the power of the human mind in comparison to the power of God in the universe. We bring this section to a close with her words regarding the renewing of our minds:

> As we think, we change the physical nature of our brain. As we consciously direct our thinking, we can wire out toxic patterns of thinking and replace

them with healthy thoughts. New thought networks grow. We increase our intelligence and bring healing to our brains, minds, and physical bodies. It all starts in the realm of the mind, with our ability to think and choose—the most powerful thing in the universe after God, and indeed, fashioned after God.[1]

CHAPTER 20:

Personal Declaration Blueprint

A Simple Approach to the Construction and Application of Your Declarations

In an effort to lay a foundation for this Personal Declaration Blueprint, I want to drill down into a couple of definitions that will establish clarity regarding the primary applications involved in this blueprint.

Definitions

1. **Declaration** (noun): A formal or explicit statement or announcement.[1]
2. **Explicit**: Plainly expressed, or that plainly expresses. Having no disguised meaning or reservation; definite; open; unreserved; too clear to be misunderstood and too emphatic to be disregarded. So plainly stated that there is no doubt.[2]

3. **Declare** (verb): To make known; To announce formally to be or exist; To assert positively.[3]

4. **Decree** (noun): [a] A formal order determining what is to be done or not to be done in a particular matter; an official order issued by a legal authority.[4]

5. **Decree** (verb): To ordain or assign by law or edict.[5]

A declaration consists of words. A declaration can be words spoken or it can be written words. There is an expression that says, "The pen is mightier than the sword." The pen may be mightier, but the voice is more powerful. And when they are combined for a declaration, that declaration is *mighty powerful!*

Right now is a perfect time to activate the power of declaring and decreeing a thing. What does this mean? It means that it is time to invoke the power of your words with authority. It is time to call the things that do not exist as if they did! In Romans 4:17, we see this is what God did, and He expects us to do the same, because this is *a Kingdom principle.*

In an effort to clarify the application of declaring and decreeing a thing and to understand the difference, consider the following description.

When you speak a declaration, you make known something emphatically, openly, or formally. When you declare something, you make it known, sometimes in the face of actual or potential contradiction. A declaration is a written or oral indication of a fact, opinion, or belief. But when your declaration is based on God's Word, it is a written or oral indication of a truth. Facts are subject to change, but the truth never changes.

A decree is an official order issued by a legal authority. Jesus has given us Spiritual Authority. A Divine Decree is taking God's Words and speaking them out, backed up by the power of the Spirit. Again, we have been given the authority from Jesus to make these decrees into our realms of influence, and as we do, it will begin to create the will of God in our life and in the lives of others in the spiritual realm.

You can begin to establish God's in your life and call things that are not as though they were with Divine Decrees.

> You will also declare a thing, And it will be established for you.
> —Job 22:28 NKJV

How to Create an Effective Declaration

Begin with a five-part construction:

1. **Make It Personal** (I, Me, My)

Personalize the declaration with language in the first person, because you are making a statement about yourself. Therefore, it's most effective when it starts with you.

For example:

> "[My] mind plans my way, but the Lord directs [my] steps."
> —See Proverbs 16:9

2. **Make It Present Tense** (Am, Is, Have)

Use wording that expresses a now time frame. Write as if you are currently receiving or experiencing that which you desire in that moment.

For example:

> "[I am] led by the Spirit of God."
> —See Romans 8:14

3. **Identify the Attribute or Specific Desire**

Specify a quality, feature, characteristic, or inherent desire that you want to become a reality or an enhanced development.

For example:

"I am wealthy and healthy, and my soul prospers."
—See 3 John 2

4. **Add Emotion to Your Declaration** (Happy, Grateful, Excited, Thankful, Blessed)

Emotion is a powerful element. Include a descriptive positive emotion in the construction of your declaration.

For example:

"I am blessed to receive unexpected checks in the mail. I receive surprise money. I have financial favor. The blessings of the Lord makes me truly rich. I am happy and grateful that money comes to me in increasing abundance on a regular and continuous basis."

5. **Include Select Support Scriptures**

Select scriptures that God has impressed upon your heart and mind that are relevant to your desire. When your declaration and God's Word and His promises align, what you declare shall come to pass.

For example:

"[I am being] transformed by the renewing of my mind."
—See Romans 12:2

"I declare that all things are working together for my good.
—See Romans 8:28

"I have the wisdom from God."
—James 1:5-8

Speaking declarations based on scriptures is very powerful.

Application Quick Tips

- Write it out. Document your declaration in writing and use it when you speak it, as in "Scripture implies. . . ." Write the vision and make it plain so when you read it, you can run with it.

- Read it out loud two to three times a day. Let your voice-print be heard and released into the atmosphere. It can be whispered or even said under your breath. You can shout it out or use a moderate volume. The main thing is to employ the power of your tongue.

- When possible and when available, try to speak softly and calmly in a quiet place.

- Begin by taking deep breaths and breathe slowly. It helps you to relax and regulate your mood.

- See your declaration delivered through eyes of faith! Employ your imagination and visualize the results you desire. It may help you to visualize by finding a picture or image that represents what you want.

- Seal it! Take a moment to thank God that He watches over His Word to perform it. As you speak your declaration, proclaim, "My words will not return to me void, but will be fruitful, and will accomplish what I have sent them to do."

- The best times to read or recite declarations that program your subconscious mind are:
    1. Right at bedtime or just before going to sleep. This gives your subconscious mind something specific to work on while you sleep.
    2. Right after you wake up in the morning or arise from sleep. These two times are when the subconscious mind is most receptive and most responsive to suggestions and programming.

    Any other time, other than these two times, will also work . . . such as lunchtime. You take that time to feed your body, so take a couple of minutes to also feed your subconscious mind. Remember, repetition also increases your belief, expectation, and faith.
- Stay positive and keep believing in the power and workings of your subconscious mind, which God designed to serve you. Trust in its divine-designed function.
- After repeating your affirmations each time, as you go through your day, you can sum it all up with a one- or two-word topical attribute such as "success" or "wealth" or "health" or "happiness," etc., quietly to yourself. These are trigger words. Your subconscious mind has already been activated by your declaration statements. So the use of one or two keywords will just reinforce the desired results.

Note: As you fall off to sleep, repeat a keyword/trigger word over and over, again and again, until you fall asleep. It's like a lullaby. But, of course, say your prayers first.

Declaration Examples

Note: Use these as you see fit. You can use them as is or modify to suit your need. You may also just use them as a template or guide in developing your own personal declaration.

- I am happy and thankful that I receive a pay raise each month.
- I am thankful I am qualified for top-tier bonus every month!
- Money is constantly circulating in my life.
- I believe I receive overflow blessing, according to Malachi 3:10.
- I am happy and thankful that I am cancer free!
- I receive unexpected checks in the mail! I receive surprise money.
- My subconscious mind serves me by the Infinite Intelligence of God!
- I am thankful for $____________ per month cash flow.
- I am so happy and thankful now that my body is healthy!
- The power of God in me heals and restores my body.
- I am so happy and grateful now that money comes to me in increasing abundance, through various sources on a continuous basis.
- I attract abundant prosperity.
- I am excited and thankful for a quick and substantial increase in my financial income now.
- My words are charged with prospering power.

- Through Infinite Intelligence within my subconscious mind, wealth is being created for me now.
- Money comes to me in avalanches of abundance.
- Wealth and riches are in my house, and my righteousness endures forever.

Voiceprints in the Atmosphere: Declarations and Professions of Faith for Your Wealth, Health, and Success

- God blesses me today, God honors me today, I am a success today, God prospers me today, God favors me today. God makes His face to shine upon me. God is gracious to me today. I have God's favor everywhere I go and in everything I do. He never leaves me nor forsakes me.
- I have the joy of the Lord as my strength. I choose to put on the garment of praise for the spirit of heaviness. I choose to praise God in all things. God, I know You inhabit the praise of Your people. So when I praise You, You come on the scene of my circumstances. And if God be for me, who then can be against me?
- I declare the blood of Jesus over my finances. I am an overcomer. I overcome by the blood of the Lamb and the Word of my testimony. Jesus is the High Priest of my confession.
- As I give, it is given to me; good measure, pressed down, shaken together, and running over, men pour into my lap.
- I do remember the Lord my God for it is He who gives me power to get wealth, that He may establish His covenant of increase in my life.

- I delight myself in the Lord, and He gives me the desires of my heart.
- Christ has redeemed me from the curse of the law. Christ has redeemed me from poverty. The Lord commands blessing upon me. For poverty, He has given me wealth. For sickness, He has given me health.
- I experience no lack, for God supplies all of my need according to His riches in glory by Christ Jesus.
- The Lord has pleasure in my prosperity, and Abraham's blessings are mine.
- I am so grateful that the Lord commands blessings upon me and in all that I set my hands to do. I am blessed in my work.
- I am redeemed and released from the bondage of debt. I subscribe to God's financial plan, and I give my way out of debt. Praise the Lord, I am debt free.
- The stronghold of debt and the mismanagement of wealth is broken from my family for generations to come.
- I call things that are not as though they were. My finances are debt free. My bills and expenses are paid. I give seed as a sower, and I have more than enough to pay my bills.
- Father, I confess daily that You have opened the good treasure of heaven and You have poured out Your blessings upon me. The works of my hands are blessed and fruitful, and all that I do prospers and comes to maturity. I am God dependent, for You furnish my prosperity in abundance and fulfill the desires of my heart. You have supplied all my needs according to Your riches in glo-

ry. I am prosperous in spirit, soul, and body. And You withhold no good thing because I walk uprightly. I am the head and not the tail; I am above and not beneath. I find favor with You and with my fellow man, for I cast my bread upon the water. I thank You now that I do not lack in any area of my life.

- I declare, by the stripes that Jesus bore for me, I am healed.
- I declare that I will live and declare the glory of God.
- I declare that my body belongs to Jesus. The Devil has no right or authority to touch my body. Every disease germ and every virus that touches me dies instantly. Every infirmity must go. Anything in or on my body that is not from God must go. I am healed, healthy, and whole, in Jesus's name.
- I declare life, health, and strength to my physical body. I am quickened by the Spirit of God. The same Spirit that raised Christ from the dead dwells in me, and it quickens and makes alive my mortal body. I declare that I have the mind of Christ, and I hold the thoughts, feelings, and purposes of His heart. My mind thinks clearly. It is not scattered nor distracted. I have divine focus, insight, and concentration.
- I declare that I have divine-inspired ideas, creative concepts, and superior strategies for business and income.
- I declare that I am proactive and lead by the Spirit of God within me.

- I declare supernatural strength in my mirage. There shall be no division in my family. We are in one accord of the same mind, with the same goal and same vision.
- I declare that this is my time for the seven-fold restoration of everything that the enemy has stolen from my life.
- I declare supernatural debt cancellation. My finances are debt free.
- I declare that I have the favor of God. I am diligent to do the will of God and to obey the Word of God. I am thankful that God will cause me to stand before great men.
- I am the righteousness of God in Christ Jesus. I receive supernatural finances as the wealth of the wicked is laid up for the just like me.
- I delight myself in the Lord, and He gives me the desires of my heart.

Remember, thoughts become things, and your words are powerful. Whatever you think about, speak of, and focus on the most expands in your life and becomes reality. Believe in the power of your personal declarations and trust in God's design of your Divine Mind.

APPENDIX 1

How Many Squares Are There?

The puzzle is a 4x4 square grid.

COUNT THE SQUARES

Notes

INTRODUCTION

1. Ariana Ayu, "Three Parts of Your Mind That Affect Your Ability to Make Decisions, " Inc., April 22, 2016, https://www.inc.com/ariana-ayu/3-parts-of-your-mind-that-affect-your-ability-to-make-decisions.html.

2. "BCV—Book, Chapter, Verse" is a term coined by Senior Pastor Michael Hankins (1949–2021).

CHAPTER 2

1. "KJV + Strong's Genesis 1," accessed September 6, 2024, https://biblehub.com/kjvs/genesis/1.htm.

CHAPTER 1

1. Wikipedia, s.v. "brain," last modified August 11, 2024, https://en.wikipedia.org/wiki/Brain.

2. Deane Alban, "72 Amazing Human Brain Facts (Based on the Latest Science)," SDBIF, last updated February 6, 2019, https://sdbif.org/72-amazing-human-brain-facts-based-on-the-latest-science/.

CHAPTER 3

1. John Kehoe, "The Six Laws of the Mind and How to Use Them," Mind Power, accessed August 11, 2024, https://www.learnmindpower.com/laws-of-the-mind/.

CHAPTER 4

1. *Google Dictionary*, s.v. "enmity," accessed September 5, 2024, https://googledictionary.freecollocation.com/meaning?word=enmity#google_vignette.

CHAPTER 5

1. *Cambridge English Dictionary,* s.v. "faith," accessed August 5, 2024, https://dictionary.cambridge.org/us/dictionary/english/faith.

2. Funk, Charles Earl, s. v. "faith," *Funk & Wagnalls New Practical Standard Encyclopedia Dictionary* (New York: Funk & Wagnalls, 1952).

CHAPTER 6

1. Montgomery F. Essig, *The Railway Through the World* (Nashville, The Southwestern Company, 1908), 232, https://www.google.com/books/edition/The_Railway_Through_the_Word/tg5ISlhiK3EC?hl=en&gbpv=1&printsec=frontcover.

2. Merriam-Webster.com, s.v. "defining moment," accessed August 21, 2024, https://www.merriam-webster.com/dictionary/defining%20moment.

3. Google English Dictionary, provided by Oxford Languages, s.v. "homogeneous," accessed August 26, 2024, https://www.google.com/search

4. Ibid.

5. *Dictionary.com,* s.v. "homogeneous," accessed August 26, 2024, https://www.dictionary.com/browse/homogeneous.

6. Ibid.

7. *Funk & Wagnalls Encyclopedia Dictionary,* s.v. "heart."

8. William Smith and Samuel W. Barnum (ed.), *Smith's Comprehensive Dictionary of the Bible,* s.v. "heart" (New York, London: D. Appleton and Company, 1901).

9. James Strong, *Strong's Expanded Exhaustive Concordance of the Bible,* s.v. "kardia" (Nashville: Thomas Nelson, 2009), 2588, https://www.bibletools.org/index.cfm/fuseaction/Lexicon.show/ID/G2588/kardia.htm.

10. Strong, *Concordance*, s.v. "leb," 3820, https://www.blueletterbible.org/lexicon/h3824/rsv/wlc/0-1/.

11. Ibid.

12. Ibid.

13. *Funk & Wagnalls Encyclopedia Dictionary,* s.v. "mind."

14. Ibid.

15. *Funk & Wagnalls Encyclopedia Dictionary,* s.v. "soul."

16. Ibid.

17. Joseph Thayer, *Thayer's Greek Lexicon,* s.v. "nous," 3563, accessed September 5, 2024, https://biblehub.com/greek/3563.htm.

18. Ibid.

19. Strong, *Concordance*, s.v. "leb," 3820, https://www.blueletterbible.org/lexicon/h3824/rsv/wlc/0-1/.

20. Strong, *Concordance*, s.v. "kardia," 2588, https://biblehub.com/greek/2588.htm.

21. Ibid.

22. Ibid.

23. *King James Bible Dictionary*, s.v. "kardia," G2588, accessed September 5, 2024, https://kingjamesbibledictionary.com/StrongsNo/G2588/hearts.

24. Strong, *Concordance*, s.v. "leb," 3820, https://www.blueletterbible.org/lexicon/h3824/rsv/wlc/0-1/.

25. Lois Tverberg, "Levav – Heart, Mind," En-Gedi Resource Center, July 1, 2015, https://engediresourcecenter.com/2015/07/01/levav-heart-mind/

26. Fred Plumer, "How Do We Know We Have a Soul?" Progressive Christianity, August 15, 2017, https://progressivechristianity.org/resource/how-do-we-know-we-have-a-soul/.

27. Strong, *Concordance*, s.v. "psuché," 5590, accessed September 5, 2024, https://biblehub.com/greek/5590.htm.

28. Ibid.

29. Strong, *Concordance*, s.v. "nephesh," 5315, accessed September 5, 2024, https://biblehub.com/hebrew/5315.htm.

CHAPTER 8

1. Wikipedia, s.v. "mind," last modified July 30, 2024, https://en.wikipedia.org/wiki/Mind.

2. Ariana Ayu, "Three Parts of Your Mind," https://www.inc.com/ariana-ayu/3-parts-of-your-mind-that-affect-your-ability-to-make-decisions.html.

3. Kendra Cherry, "What Is the Automatic Nervous System?" Verywell Mind, updated May 9, 2023, https://www.verywellmind.com/what-is-the-autonomic-nervous-system-2794823.

4. *Funk & Wagnalls Encyclopedia Dictionary,* s.v. "subconscious."

5. Ibid.

6. See Gail Marra, "Nine Interesting Facts about Your Subconscious Mind," Gail Marra Hypnotherapy, November 11, 2021, https://www.gailmarrahypnotherapy.com/9-interesting-facts-about-your-subconscious-mind/.

7. *Cambridge Dictionary,* s.v. "belief," accessed August 23, 2024, https://dictionary.cambridge.org/us/dictionary/english/belief.

8. Alok Jha, "Where Belief Is Born," The Guardian, June 30, 2005, https://www.theguardian.com/science/2005/jun/30/psychology.neuroscience#:~:text=Halligan%20says%20that%20belief%20takes,the%20world%2C%22%20he%20says.

9. Ibid.

10. Sathyanarayana Rao, T.S.; Asha, M. R.1; Jagannatha Rao, K. S.2; Vasudevaraju, P.2, "The Biochemistry of Belief," *Indian*

Journal of Psychiatry 51(4):p 239-241, Oct–Dec 2009. | DOI: 10.4103/0019-5545.58285.

11. Ibid.

12. Mandie Holgate, "Seven Ways to Break Boundaries and Self-Imposed Limits," LifeHack, December 8, 2020. https://www.lifehack.org/890717/break-boundaries.

13. Wikipedia, "Apollo PGNCS," June 7, 2024, https://en.wikipedia.org/wiki/Apollo_PGNCS.

14. Kelly Locker, "Seven Mind Mastery Principles to Harness the Power of the Subconscious Mind, Happy Brain Counseling, October 7, 2018, https://happy-brain.com/newsletters/7-mind-mastery-principles-to-harness-the-power-of-the-subconscious-mind/.

15. Chris Mosunic (reviewer), "How Long Does It Take to Create a Habit (And How to Do It)?, Calm, accessed August 18, 2024, https://www.calm.com/blog/how-long-does-it-take-to-create-a-habit#:~:text=Maxwell%20Maltz's%20work%20in%20the,guaranteed%20period%20for%20habit%20alteration.

CHAPTER 9

1. Wikipedia, "Loose Lips Sink Ships," last modified August 6, 2024, https://en.wikipedia.org/wiki/Loose_lips_sink_ships.

CHAPTER 10

1. Joseph Murphy, "The Power of Your Subconscious Mind – Joseph Murphy, Chapter 3 – The Miracle Working Power of Your Subconscious – Part 1," LingQ, accessed September 5, 2024, https://www.lingq.com/en/learn-english-online/courses/233550/chapter-3-the-miracle-working-power-of-743864/#:~:text=William%20James%2C%20the%20father%20of,called%20the%20law%20of%20life.

2. David Whitehead and Sue Bingham, “Habit Formation and Learning in Young Children,” University of Cambridge, Money Advice Service, 2013, tinyurl.com/mr9bmkay.

3. *Merriam-Webster.com,* s.v. “belief,” accessed August 10, 2024, https://www.merriam-webster.com/dictionary/belief.

CHAPTER 11

1. Stuart I. Rochester, *The Battle Behind Bars: Navy and Marine POWs in the Vietnam War* (Washington, DC: Naval History & Heritage Command in partnership with the Naval Historical Foundation, 2010), https://www.history.navy.mil/content/dam/nhhc/research/publications/publication-508-pdf/BatBehindBars_508.pdf.

2. *Oxford English Dictionary,* s.v. “synergistic,” https://www.oed.com/search/dictionary/?scope=Entries&q=synergistic.

CHAPTER 12

1. *Dictionary.com*, s.v. “repetition,” https://www.dictionary.com/browse/repetition.

CHAPTER 13

1. See Dinesh Ramoo, “2.2 The Articulatory System,” Psychology of Language©, https://opentextbc.ca/psyclanguage/chapter/the-articulatory-system/.

2. Patricia T. O’Conner and Stewart Kellerman, “Let There Be Light,” Grammarphobia (blog), March 18, 2015, https://www.grammarphobia.com/blog/2015/03/let-there-be-light.html#:~:text=A%20word%20for%20word%20translation,ve%20added%20capitalization%20and%20punctuation.

3. “KJV + Strong’s Genesis 1,” https://biblehub.com/kjvs/genesis/1.htm.

4. LucyD, “What Are the Earth’s Harmonic Resonate Frequencies?” Sciencing, updated April 25, 2017, https://sciencing.com/earths-harmonic-resonate-frequencies-8600773.html.

5. “Sound,” Science World, accessed August 23, 2024, https://www.scienceworld.ca/resource/sound/.

6. The Voice Foundation, “Understanding How Voice Is Produced,” accessed August 12, 2024, https://voicefoundation.org/health-science/voice-disorders/anatomy-physiology-of-voice-production/understanding-voice-production/.

7. *Merriam-Webster.com*, s.v. “voiceprint,” accessed August 10, 2024, https://www.merriam-webster.com/dictionary/voiceprint#:~:text=%3A%20an%20individually%20distinctive%20pattern%20of%20certain%20voice%20characteristics%20that%20is%20spectrographically%20produced.

8. Rana King, “The Wonders of Voice through Voiceprint Technology,” Voice Over Herald.com, May 19, 2015, https://www.voiceoverherald.com/the-wonders-of-voice-through-voiceprint-technology/.

CHAPTER 14

1. *Wicktionary.com*, s.v. “state of mind,” last updated August 25, 2024, https://en.wiktionary.org/wiki/state_of_mind.

2. *American Heritage Dictionary of the English Language*, s.v. “mindset,” https://www.thefreedictionary.com/mindset.

3. Jesse Wisnewski, “Bible Verses About Money: Nine Biblical Principles of Money & Possessions,” Tithe.ly, accessed September 5, 2024, get.tithe.ly/blog/bible-verses-about-money.

4. Ibid.

5. Ibid.

6. *YourDictionary*, s.v. “mindset,” https://www.yourdictionary.com/mindset.

CHAPTER 17

1. Karolina Hübner, “Spinoza’s Epistemology and Philosophy of Mind,” *The Stanford Encyclopedia of Philosophy* (Spring 2022

Edition), Edward N. Zalta (ed.), URL = <https://plato.stanford.edu/archives/spr2022/entries/spinoza-epistemology-mind/>.

2. John A. Bargh, "How Unconscious Thought and Perception Affect Our Every Waking Moment," *Scientific American,* January 1, 2014, https://www.scientificamerican.com/article/how-unconscious-thought-and-perception-affect-our-every-waking-moment/.

CHAPTER 19

1. Caroline Leaf, *Switch on Your Brain: The Key to Peak Happiness, Thinking, and Health* (Ada, MI: Baker Books, 2015.

CHAPTER 20

1. *Collins Dictionary*, s.v. "declaration," https://www.collinsdictionary.com/us/dictionary/english/declaration.

2. *Funk and Wagnalls Encyclopedia Dictionary,* s.v. "explicit."

3. *Funk & Wagnalls Encyclopedia Dictionary*, s.v. "declare."

4. *Funk & Wagnalls Encyclopedia Dictionary,* s.v. "decree."

5. *Legal Dictionary,* s.v. "decree," https://legaldictionary.net/decree/.

6. *Funk & Wagnalls Encyclopedia Dictionary,* s.v. "decree (verb)."

About the Author

Thomas Lacy has invested more than forty years studying and researching spiritual and scientific laws of the mind. He has practiced the combination of truth found in scripture and the facts of mental science. Mr. Lacy has been serving in church ministry for over sixty years. He has also been in church leadership roles for over thirty years and has provided family financial counseling for decades. He is a master certified financial coach and a seasoned personal financial analyst. He and his wife, Dr. Constance Lacy, are Ordained Elders in their local church.

Mr. Lacy grew up in the home of his parents, who were the senior pastors of the church. He is also a retired award-winning engineer for a Fortune 100 technology company. He has had a successful career in financial services as a senior regional manager for one of America's major financial service companies.

The content of this book has been the springboard for his success and achievements. Mr. Lacy's prayer is that this book will have a profound impact on the reader's life for the glory of God and service to humankind.

For teaching and speaking engagements,
please contact

Thomas Lacy

Mr.LacySpeaks@gmail.com

Requesting Your Help Please

If you have enjoyed reading *How A Divine Mind Works,* would you mind taking a moment to write a review on Amazon? Even a short review helps. Just a couple of sentences. I am grateful for your support, and it will mean a lot to me.

If someone you care about is dealing with worry, debt, stress, or could benefit from understanding how to think right for their success in life, please send them a copy of this book. You can gift it to them as an investment in their life, or recommend they get a copy. I sincerely want them to grow and benefit from the content.

If you would like to order copies of this book for your company employees, school, group or organization, please go to ThomasLacy.com and use the "BUY" button.